Ben Peterson
Proverbs 22:1

Road to GOLD

Ben and John Peterson's 1972 Olympic Journey

By: Ben Peterson

Road to Gold

For information address: Ben Peterson
Camp of Champs Publications
PO Box 222
Watertown, WI 53094
920-261-8071

Printed in the United States of America

ISBN: 978-0-692-57297-9

First Edition

Consultant: Mike Chapman
Compiled by: Phil Peterson
Edited by: Andy Peterson, Jan Peterson
Cover Design: Rick Vogeney, Light Craft Graphics, Inc.
Page Layout: Angie Hardenbrook

A good name is rather to be chosen than great riches,
and loving favor rather than silver and gold.

Proverbs 22:1

Table of Contents

FOREWORDS

It is a great honor to be asked to write the foreword for this amazing book, *Road to Gold: Ben and John Peterson's 1972 Olympic Journey.* I have attended 45 NCAA tournaments, two Olympics and three World Wrestling Championships, and so I have known most of the great wrestlers in American history of the last half century, and I am in awe of what the Peterson brothers have accomplished and what they stand for as athletes and men. That is true off the mat as well as on the mat.

John and Ben grew up humble and hard working on a farm in a small Wisconsin community, but they had the advantage of living with two tremendous role models – their mother and father. The early parts of this book will provide the reader with a sense of what it means to be totally connected to one's family and dedicated to the values taught by such remarkable people.

Writing with clarity and candor, Ben takes the reader on an odyssey of growth in spirit and productivity that is rarely seen in America these days. The book reveals the work ethic that has served this family so incredibly well, and that played a key role in America's emergence as the greatest society ever devised by man.

The underlying theme of the book is the family's total commitment to a deep and abiding Christian faith. Time after time, Ben tells us how he managed to move past roadblocks and overcome setbacks as he struggled his way up the ladder of success. His journey was fueled by an unwavering faith in Jesus Christ and his belief in the values taught by his parents and stressed by them on a daily basis.

The author discusses his innermost feelings at crucial times and reveals just how fragile the human spirit can be – even for men destined to become Olympic champions.

While this is primarily Ben and John's story, the reader will also meet the other members of the family, including older brothers who inspired them and enabled them to reach their full potential by pushing and cajoling them. Along the way, you will join Ben as he makes his way to Ames, Iowa, one of the citadels of wrestling royalty, and comes under the influence of two of the finest coaches in college sports history – Harold Nichols and Les Anderson. You will also meet a cast of legendary figures, such as Dan Gable, Bobby Douglas, Tom Peckham, Carl Adams, Chuck Jean, and many more.

Road to Gold is not just a book about wrestling or a book about sports but, rather, a primer on life itself… an educational treatise on how to gain stunning successes by paying attention to what matters most. It is, in essence, a book about winning in life, at every level. I cannot recommend it highly enough and believe it should find a home on the bookshelf of every wresting fan in America.

Mike Chapman
Author of 27 books
Founder of WIN magazine, the Dan Hodge Trophy, and the International Wrestling Institute and Museum (now the National Hall of Fame Dan Gable Museum)

An amazing read. The recollections are astounding. The insights are so valuable to all. The ability to move forward always helps. Living your life in positive faith-based ways is good. That's what this book is and it reminds me of why I became attached to these Peterson brothers – Ben and John. They help keep one "in line" and the disciplines they bring to one's life are never forgotten. Of course, it doesn't hurt to stay connected with these disciplines in your everyday life to help keep your everyday life very meaningful.

Ben Peterson is very unique but this book helped me understand him. I always wondered how he "lasted" in certain circles of life, being he was so disciplined in his lifestyle. This reading taught me that he could adjust to others even though they were not what he believed in. Or even if he didn't, he would learn for the next time to handle it better or in another way.

This read shows us that we all can be unique and that with the right beliefs and attitude most anything is possible. Follow Ben and his remarkable journey in becoming an Olympic Champion Wrestler and how he developed his strong Christian Faith during his early years of humble beginnings. To develop and make accomplishments of this magnitude is rare, but the process is explained well and most will gain an understanding that can make a difference in their lives.

The Petersons, Ben and John are leaders. Yes, they needed others to help lead them, but with that direction they made unbelievable strides. Because of this they have affected masses of others for the good. Read and study this very good book and let them help you become better.

Dan Gable
World and Olympic Champion
Legendary Coach of the Iowa Hawkeyes
Continual promoter for wrestling

ENDORSEMENTS

For over 3 decades I have known Ben and John Peterson as coaches, friends, mentors, and role models. Knowing them has been one of the great privileges of my life and finer men of character I have never met. The countless hours listening to their captivating stories of struggle, success, faith, and family profoundly impacted me as they brought me into their worlds, into their thoughts, and into their journeys. *Road to Gold* is an excellent compilation of those stories that invite the reader to an inner look at the heart of two American champions. I highly recommend this book to anyone who is not only curious about what makes a great champion but more importantly what makes great men.

Mike Houck
Husband, Father, Grandpa, Teacher, and Coach
America's 1st Greco-Roman World Champion

The wrestling world has admired the Peterson brothers since their Olympic Gold performances in the '70s. In this book, Ben Peterson takes us inside preparation for the Olympics and shows the intensity with which Dan Gable, the Peterson brothers, and other team members pushed themselves to be the best in the world. After reading the first half of this book, you will better understand the importance of strong family support and values for any true success in life. And even more importantly, by the end of the book you will know that there is more to life than winning.

Ben and John Peterson inspire me. They are true champions full of grit and determination and, most of all, always pointing to a greater gold: the lasting rewards that come from knowing and loving Jesus Christ as Savior and Lord. I highly recommend *Road to Gold.*

Tim Johnson
Vice President of Field Ministries FCA Midwest Region
"The Voice of College Wrestling" ESPN & The Big Ten Network (BTN)
Member, National Wrestling Hall of Fame

We live in a society that desperately needs to have "heroes." Every group and avenue in life has these people... the sport of wrestling offers Ben and John Peterson as two such heroes.

After reading *Road to Gold*, I am not only affected as a wrestler but on several other fronts. There are many who would benefit from reading *Road to Gold*:

- All ages of student athletes... how to overcome setbacks and dream of greater things and the next gold medal!
- Parents... how to raise, encourage and support your children in whatever it is they find themselves straining towards!
- Believers in themselves and in Christ... how your beliefs may not always be popular or convenient, but to remain strong in those beliefs.
- Coaches... of any sport... how to understand the knowledge, wisdom, and influence you possess!

You will enjoy learning the foundation of what made Ben and John the very best in the world at what they do, and along the way pick up lessons on how to be a better version of yourself. I know I did. It is a story that needs to be told. Thank you, Ben!

Tim Fader
Former Coach at UW LaCrosse and UW Whitewater
UW Eau Claire Head Wrestling Coach

I am one of thousands of kids who sat on a mat at Camp of Champs® listening and being motivated by Ben & John's stories. Thirty years later, I can still remember them like it was yesterday and I find myself repeating them to those I coach. *Road to Gold* now makes those stories and many more available to motivate, mentor, and inspire wrestlers. Every coach would benefit greatly from reading this book and by making it required reading for their athletes.

Dan Willis
Coach, Chicago Hope Academy
Chicago, IL

I could write a recommendation for *Road to Gold* without ever reading the book because of the 30 years spent being mentored by Ben and John Peterson. I have heard their stories and was challenged as a young man, and continue to be challenged, to attack tests and overcome limitations. Ben and John's lives have significantly improved the lives of those around them, and I am a better husband, father, and wrestler because of them. However, having read *Road to Gold* allows me to recommend the book as a wonderful account of the life and journey of two men who struggled to the top of Olympic wrestling and then used that success to be significant men who have transformed lives.

Jim Gruenwald
2-time Olympian
Wheaton College Head Wrestling/Strength & Conditioning Coach

PREFACE

Writing a book about yourself and others is a risky undertaking. You take the chance of being misunderstood. You risk getting the facts wrong and making yourself and others look better or worse than what is true. Ben has bravely taken that risk. He has the added risk of knowing that I, being an older brother, am a big part of his story. He knows I do not always remember events the same way he does. We have discussed many things together over the years and I am so grateful we can still be good friends even if we don't always agree. I guess that is why we were able to make each other better on the mat. We were fierce competitors in the practice room and yet never ended up fighting against each other. You will learn how God worked in my life at a young age to help curb my aggressive nature. It has been a long process and God is still working on me.

For people to accomplish great things, many events and people need to cross their paths at the right times and places. Ben has written about events and people in a way that encourages and inspires. He also writes about the many things that helped us to accomplish what we did at the highest level of wrestling. He has written that no two paths to becoming an Olympic champion are the same. His story and my story run parallel with one another. At times they intersect for a short while and sometimes appear to follow the same path. At other times our stories contrast to such extremes they seem to be going in opposite directions. Ben wrestled varsity competition all four years in high school. I wrestled just two years on varsity. Ben qualified twice for the state tournament. I failed to qualify at all. Ben attended Iowa State University when they had the best college wrestling program in the country. I attended an NAIA school that had a slightly better-than-average wrestling program but no longer even has wrestling! Ben was a three-time All American and a two-time Division 1 national champion. I finally became an All American, placing 5th as a senior. Reading this book will help answer the question: How could someone place 2nd in the Olympics just five years after failing to qualify for the high school state tournament?

I trust you will find this book as interesting as I have. It kept my attention for six hours straight. And that was without the pictures! There are so many factors that prepared us for the Olympics. Ben does a good job in describing those events in a way that allows the reader to learn important lessons.

In the Bible, God gives us a promise that He works all things together for the good of those who love Him and are called according to His purpose. Ben relates how God's hand can be seen in the events that took place and through the people who were so important in helping us get to Munich. I was brought to tears more than once as I read how he describes the influence that our brother, Phil, and Dan Gable had on us. It is so true that without Dan we would never have made it to Munich, let alone won medals! Thank you Dan! I have often stated that without my wife Nancy, the best I could do was second place! Nancy, you helped me make it one step higher four years later! Thank you, Nanc! That part of the story will have to wait for another book.

I am so grateful that God has blessed us by enabling us to be Olympians. There are many wrestlers who were better than we were and yet we were given the opportunity to be on the stand. Thank you, Lord! I pray that as you read our stories you will be pointed to the Lord Jesus. He died for us so that we could know Him and make Him known. I trust you are able to see His work in our lives through the stories that unfold. As you read this book, it is my prayer that God, in a special way, will use our stories to call you into a relationship with Himself. If you already know Him, it is my prayer that this book will encourage you to grow in that relationship.

John Peterson
Ben's older brother

ACKNOWLEDGEMENTS

Thank you to the many friends that listened to our stories and then encouraged me to write them down. The staff and board members of Camp of Champs® urged me a thousand times.

Then Mike Chapman began asking me to write for WIN Magazine. As my writing confidence grew, the idea of a biography grew. Bryan Van Kley has continued that encouragement. Mike has repeatedly rehearsed the steps for completing this project. Thank you, Mike and Bryan.

While writing many stories for WIN, there was still no structure of a book. During a three-hour phone conversation with my oldest brother, Phil, I expressed my desire to put the articles into book form. He agreed to take all my random stories and put them in sequence order so we could see what was done and what was missing. Thank you, Phil, for showing me that a book was in all those stories.

My son, Andy, did the first major step of proofing and editing. We hope to work together on future projects. Jan, my typist and proofer for thirty-six-plus years, attacked "our book" making it much smoother and more readable. Thank you, Andy and Jan.

Also I must acknowledge my family, coaches, teammates, and especially John. Without your wise decisions and hard work the story would never have happened. John and I did not achieve Olympic medals in our own corner. It was a family project from the start.

Finally, I credit the change that Jesus Christ has made in our lives. From the time John stood up and trusted Him as a twelve year old boy, we have been on a different trajectory. My similar choice two years later bonded us on a journey for eternity which has made some stops along the way to pick up some gold nuggets.

INTRODUCTION

No two people will have the same path to a task as complex as winning Olympic medals. Yet there are many common difficulties and heights everyone must navigate.

Winning the Olympics is not an exact science and every Olympian's story is unique, just like your life is unique. Our road was neither simple nor direct. This is the story of the people and the many events that together set the stage for us to compete on the biggest stage in the wrestling world.

I invite you to join John and me as I explain our journey. Whether you want to learn how to travel your own *Road to GOLD* or just want to enjoy ours, I know you will be energized by our experiences.

Thank you for joining us on our journey to GOLD.

Ben Peterson

Early Experiences

—1— NOT ASHAMED OF SMALL BEGINNINGS

We were raised in a large family: Mom, Dad, Phil, Tom, Becky, John, me, and Dan. And until I was eight, our grandmother lived with us also. We were all born and raised near tiny unincorporated Comstock amid the rolling hills of dairy farm land in northwestern Wisconsin.

Many think John and I are twins. However, John is a year and eight months older than me. We spent a lot of time playing and working together: first on our family's eighty-acre dairy farm a mile from Comstock, and then in many other places around the world.

We attended the same two-room Comstock School which had two teachers for about fifty students in grades 1-8. Since we were about a year apart in age, we were only a grade apart in school. For most of our elementary years we were taught by the same teacher.

John and I did farm work for our dad and neighboring farmers. And we loved to build things! We built a calf barn, a two-car garage, constructed and installed the cabinets in our kitchen, re-roofed our house, assembled a workshop in the basement, and stacked hay and straw in the barn. For fun we constructed forts, snow tunnels, imaginary buildings, and much more. From the beginning we planned and built together and our parents provided a healthy atmosphere in which to learn, grow, and build.

John and I regularly attended Sunday School, and we went to vacation Bible school for a week each summer. We also went away to Bible camp for a week which was the highlight of every summer.

Our camp experiences gave us an appreciation for getting away from everyday life to focus on something different. This prepared us for many U.S. training camps to come and also for our own Camp of Champs® Wrestling Camp where we have trained thousands of young wrestlers.

Mom and Dad had not traveled more than a few hundred miles away from their birthplaces, but their children's activities would take them halfway around the world.

Our oldest brother, Phil, attended the University of Wisconsin and played varsity football for the Badgers as a guard on the offensive line. He earned first-team All Big-Ten Academic honors as a senior.

After Phil came Tom who enlisted in the U.S. Army. He got our family thinking about far-away places like South Korea where he served for much of his three years of active duty.

Our only sister, Becky, took us to Chicago where she received her nurse's training.

John and I traveled across the nation and eventually around the world to wrestle.

Our younger brother, Dan, followed me to Iowa State University as a student and as a wrestler.

Mom and Dad, and other members of our family, traveled to watch us compete in places as diverse as suburban Chicago; Auburn, Alabama; and the Maryland suburbs of Washington, D.C. Later they would travel to the Olympic Games in Munich, Germany, and Montreal, Canada.

But before any of this traveling began, all of us were busy with everyday life. Mostly, we were content to stay right where we were: together at home in Comstock.

Childhood Games

Phil was an athlete from the start and a true competitor. As John and I grew up, Phil laid a foundation for us to compete in athletics by making it mostly fun. As soon and as often as he could, Phil threw a baseball, playing catch by the hour with anyone willing to play with him. He was five and a half years older than me and mature for his age. He was a big kid, even in sixth grade. As I remember it, we younger ones pretty much had to do whatever he said. To be honest, John and I did not always appreciate it when he made us hit the baseball to him for fielding practice. Phil would stand near the barn to keep our wild hits from going too far. Then when we had had enough, we hit the baseball as far as we could over the barn. While Phil was retrieving the ball, we would disappear. Of course we knew we would probably pay dearly for it later.

We still have fond memories of the "real baseball field" Phil put together in our backyard. It had bleachers, a press box, a backstop, two dug-outs, and chalk for marking the foul lines and batters' boxes. It featured a raised pitcher's mound because the field was on a hill that hid home plate from the outfielders. The field was pretty advanced considering Phil was in junior high when he built all this. I was too young to do much of anything except help dig the dugouts using an old silver spoon.

One day, Phil's build-it-out-of-whatever-materials-I-can-find mentality came to a sudden halt. Working hard to bring night baseball to Comstock, he tried to add electric lights to the field. While attempting to do this with an extension cord, Phil got an electric shock. This immediately stopped everything, and he ran at top speed toward the house yelling, "I'm dead! I'm dead! I'm dead!"

One fall day while Phil was gone, we three younger boys decided a nearby apple tree would supply several buckets of "baseballs" for batting practice. Of course when batting practice was over, smashed apples were everywhere. It never occurred to us Phil might not like seeing his field in such a mess. He did not like it at all, and we reused our apple pails to clean up the shattered apples. As we look back at what was then our real baseball field, we all chuckle because the entire thing, outfield and all, was about the size of a softball infield.

Next, we added a basketball court. Since we lived six miles from any schoolyard or playground, we built our own. What better place for a basketball court than the empty hayloft in our dairy barn! We cleared an area and stacked the remaining hay and straw bales off to one side. Phil mounted a basket with the rim and backboard extending out from the wall so that we could shoot layups. We spent many Saturday and Sunday afternoons from lunchtime until supper playing out there.

While fighting for the ball and jumping high for rebounds, we knocked out some of the wall boards and damaged several floorboards. Soon, the floor was patched and uneven. No wonder we Peterson brothers never developed the athletic ease and finesse needed to excel in basketball. But we sure learned to play "barn ball!"

Later, when Phil got serious about high school football, we had to have our own football field. He looked at one of Dad's freshly cut hayfields and said, "All we need now is to mark the boundaries and the yard lines!" Using the lawnmower to mow the grass to different heights took care of that. The only problem was, Dad still needed to have the hay grow back to feed the cows. As a result, our seasonal football field was usually short-lived.

Phil started his basement weight room about the time John and I started high school. This project was more serious because Phil was now in college. But, more on that later.

After a while, Dan added a tennis court and a 3-hole golf course to the "Peterson Sports Complex."

Our early competitions with Phil also included a day for boxing; we made our own boxing ring with corner posts and ropes. Dan was feisty but smaller than John and me, so to compensate for the size difference we boxed with him while down on our knees. We laughed until our sides ached even while trying to box with each other. Dan loved it! He bounced around the ring and hit us hard many times. Phil was the ref and also our coach. He, too, was having a good time.

A day or two later, boxing was prohibited by Mom. Why? While giving Dan his bath, she found his chest peppered with black and blue marks. Our glove-less knuckles had caused them. Phil found some old gloves and assured Mom we would use them. I don't think she ever gave her approval, and boxing on the Peterson farm came to a screeching halt.

Consistent Examples

A key element of our youth was the consistency of our parents and learning about life on the farm. Crops and seasons brought a regular yearly routine. On a daily basis, there was the requirement to milk the cows in the morning and again at night. Never in the fifteen years I watched Dad farm did he miss milking them twice a day. I also never saw him miss work at the feed mill except when he injured the end of his finger and had to go to the hospital.

Mom worked in our home the same way. She washed clothes on Mondays and Thursdays, cleaned the house on Fridays, baked on Saturdays, and prepared a great dinner every Sunday. I could set my schedule by her activities.

Along with the regular things I was expected to do when I was ten and eleven, Mom encouraged me to read the Bible every day. She said to start out with ten verses. That would take only a few minutes so I did it right before bed. After starting and stopping several times during the first year, it became a regular habit for me. Knowing that Mom, Dad, and my older siblings were working to do the same was helpful. Not much was said about it: just occasional encouragements.

Daily reading the Bible is the most stabilizing habit in my life. What I have learned from the Scriptures, and what I have learned about myself in doing this, has been invaluable to me.

I still read every morning and am thankful to learn new things about God and His Word.

An Ordinary Childhood

I tell these stories as a reminder not to downplay or discredit humble beginnings. We often have serious limitations and major difficulties that must be overcome to reach our goals. John and I learned to make the most of our limited circumstances. Phil learned this first, passed it on to us, and we built on it.

Our parents gave us a wonderful heritage and opportunities to learn. They taught us to look forward and work hard toward a better tomorrow, just as they themselves had done. They did this not only through life's joys and successes, but also through life's disappointments and failures. Our parents showed us this by their everyday example more than by any words they spoke.

You may wonder how people who grow up in ordinary circumstances can accomplish so much. Often, it is their confidence and solid goals combined with smart and hard work to achieve those goals. When they take the time to develop and combine confidence with work, things will get better for them. This keeps them, and often those around them, going during the tough times.

Do not be ashamed of your small beginnings, and do not lose hope for the future. Always work hard and work smart, doing your best to see how far your God-given talent can take you. Do not settle for just getting by.

—2—

"NO SON OF MINE WILL EVER WRESTLE!"

Other than "wrestling around" in our upstairs hallway, backyard, or dairy barn, neither John nor I knew much about true competitive wrestling until after we started high school.

In his freshman and sophomore years at Cumberland High School, Phil had played basketball as his winter sport. But Tom, who was a year younger than Phil, decided basketball would not be his winter sport. Coming from our two-room country school, almost everything in high school was new for a country boy like Tom. When one of his freshmen football teammates talked to him about wrestling, Tom was interested and decided to give it a try.

Tom came home from school and announced to Mom and Dad that he planned to try out for the Cumberland wrestling team. Mom responded forcefully, "No son of mine will ever wrestle!"

Why was she so negative about any of her boys wrestling? Mostly, it was because all she knew about wrestling was the phony vulgarity of "professional wrestling." Just the thought of her sons participating in that sort of wrestling was more than she could accept. Tom was not being very respectful to Mom and Dad at the time, and this new activity appeared to be more disrespect. Years later, when I asked Mom about her first thoughts, she described an event she had experienced years before. Apparently at the invitation of a few tavern owners, pro-wrestling had come for one night to Cumberland, Mom's hometown. A wrestling ring was set up in a side street and traffic was blocked off. The tavern doors were opened and a drunken-brawl atmosphere developed. When she described this setting to me, I immediately understood why she reacted so negatively. She wanted her sons to have nothing to do with anything that would bring them into this sort of atmosphere. Tom recalls Mom saying, "I don't want my boys fighting." It took her a while to see a wrestling match as anything other than a street fight.

Although Dad wished Tom would choose to play basketball, he began to discuss wrestling with his coworkers at the two feed mills in Cumberland and Comstock. He wondered how our high school could promote and teach the gross disrespect of professional wrestling. Through talking with others he learned high school wrestling was not done in a ring, but, rather, on a wrestling mat. He learned there was no punching, kicking, or biting allowed. High school wrestling was a safe and competitive athletic contest and was regulated by the Wisconsin Interscholastic Athletic Association (WIAA) like the other high school sports. So Dad signed Tom's permission slip allowing him to go out for the Cumberland Beavers wrestling team.

We All Learn About Wrestling

Dad began attending Tom's home wrestling meets and told Mom, "Esther, it's really not what you think. Wrestling will be good for Tom. It'll keep him busy and involved in school." Yet, we younger boys were not taken to any of Tom's matches for over a year. I guess Mom did not want to lose any more of her sons to wrestling. So the rest of us continued to play basketball by the hour in the barn. Yet in our own way, we were learning to wrestle by the physical combative way we always played "barn ball."

I'm uncertain when John and I first started wrestling in the hayloft of our barn. Becky was two years ahead of John in school and was occasionally put in charge of her three younger brothers. She was the official and our coach, pairing us off against each other. We did not know much about wrestling, that's for sure. But we enjoyed it enough to put up with the hay chaff that always seemed to stick to us and made us itch all over.

John recalls that occasionally when our parents were away, we would drag a couple old mattresses down from the attic and put them in our upstairs hallway. We used the mattresses for wrestling matches. Sometimes Dan would wrestle with us too, and Becky would oversee all this confusion. We often posted a guard at the stairway window to let us know when Mom and Dad were driving up the road. After all, we needed a little extra time to haul the mattresses back up into the attic and make it look like we had been doing something a little less rowdy than wrestling in the hallway.

John was the first of us three younger boys to go with Dad to Tom's matches, and he liked what he saw. Given his small size, John began thinking about a future for himself in wrestling. Tom would come home from practice and show him some of the basic moves he had learned. John particularly remembers being in our stairway landing and having Tom show him a half-nelson, a switch, and a deep-waist ride. From the beginning, John was fascinated with the complexity of wrestling and its many ways to take down, control, and pin an opponent.

Then without much warning, Phil decided basketball would no longer be his winter sport either. About a week into the season he joined the wrestling team. That year Mom's wrestling fears increased; now she had two sons wrestling! Any thoughts she had about her boys playing basketball for the same high school she had graduated from twenty-five years earlier were slipping away. Why would Tom and Phil want to wrestle anyway? And were all five of her sons now headed down this same path?

Our Whole Family Is Interested in Wrestling

Mom soon joined Dad and started going to Tom and Phil's wrestling matches. I can only imagine the sheepishness with which she must have entered the gym to see her first wrestling meet. I'm sure Mom, half hidden behind Dad, found an obscure seat and quietly began to watch.

Mom never did much cheering, leaving that to Dad. Instead, she would watch everything and carefully analyzed every aspect of the meets: the wrestlers, coaches, referees, and fans. But mostly she watched her sons. She soon agreed with Dad that "wrestling is good for our boys," as he had been telling her for over a year. Mom went to every home wrestling meet and tournament, and regularly prayed for her sons as they wrestled. Mom became an essential part of our wrestling. She just needed a little more time to move beyond her earlier fears.

I must emphasize I'm thankful for Mom's honesty about all this because when she saw the true competitive nature of high school wrestling and its value as a sport, she moved beyond all her earlier negative thoughts. She and Dad became our two biggest fans. Over the years, they were an enormous encouragement to us. We could not have done what we did in wrestling without them.

Dad was a patient man. He did not push Mom or insist she agree with him about wrestling, and it was now clear that all their boys were itching to wrestle. Dad saw the competitiveness in all of us. From our earliest years, Dad noticed Tom and Phil and us younger Peterson boys wanting to compete in something worthwhile. The truth was, we needed to compete in something challenging or we might get into mischief. What better way for us to compete than by participating in a safe, healthy, well organized high school wrestling match?

Dad attended school for seven years. He went to the same two-room country school in Comstock that all his children attended. Dad skipped seventh grade because he was the only student in his class. He was assigned to the eighth grade instead. Dad did not attend high school at all. Although he was a sports fan and interested in local high school sports, major league baseball, and college and professional football, he had few opportunities to compete himself. But he saw his sons having great opportunities to compete in athletics far beyond his own limited experience. Wrestling became a good thing to Mom and Dad. Together, they watched their sons compete and learn about something new that would turn out to be terrific for their whole family.

Dad was our biggest wrestling fan and Mom was a real promoter for the sport. After John and I returned from the 1972 and 1976 Olympics with our gold and silver medals, Mom was occasionally asked to speak to church and community groups. People would often ask her how she and Dad had raised two Olympic champions, and what it was like to be our Mom. When I asked her what she told them, she simply said to me, "I tell them, 'Let your sons wrestle! It'll be good for them.'"

Long after John and I graduated from high school, Mom and Dad continued to attend Cumberland's wrestling meets and post-season tournaments until Dad's death in 1990. They kept us updated on how "our" high school team was doing.

When Tom began wrestling, he had no idea what he started.

He opened the door to a big part of what our family enjoyed together over the years. Tom paved the way for the rest of us. By the time John and I entered high school, it was just assumed we would wrestle and we both looked forward to it. Later, Dan easily followed us down the same path.

All this is just part of our story: a story of how two Olympic wrestling champions came from a family where my first memories of wrestling were my mother intently saying, "No son of mine will ever wrestle!"

—3—

BROKEN, BUT NOT CRUSHED

Dan Gable, Olympic champion and highly successful wrestling coach, often talks to young athletes about the "markers" we have in life. Although a marker may seem to have nothing to do with wrestling at the time, **that marker may help make us who we are and may guide us to do something extraordinary in life.**

One of those markers hit me hard when I was in junior high school. At the time, it brought me nothing but pain, disappointment, and discouragement. Looking back on it all, I can see that much was gained from it. It helped both John and me later as we worked together on our quest toward the Olympics.

It all began at summer Bible camp on Lake Chetek, thirty-five miles southeast of our home. As we grew up, all six Peterson children attended Camp Chetek. Beginning at age nine, we swam and played softball, tetherball, ping pong, shuffleboard, and more for a whole week. These were activities we did not have much time for on a dairy farm with its unending daily chores, so it was a special treat to have a whole week to enjoy them without interruption.

We attended Camp Chetek each summer because of our parents' strong Christian faith. As the son of a Swedish immigrant, Dad grew up going to the Swedish Lutheran Church in Cumberland. During his confirmation classes in his mid-teens, he understood that Jesus Christ paid the penalty for his sins. Dad would tell us about trusting Jesus for forgiveness from those sins. And he told us that in his late twenties he gained full confidence in that forgiveness when his older brother, Walford, urged him to take God at His Word and simply believe God's promises. Dad found John 3:16; John 5:24; Romans 6:23; and Romans 10:13 very helpful. When Mom was twenty-one, and working as a sales clerk in the drugstore in Cumberland, she heard this same gospel message from the pastor's wife of Dad's church. She also accepted Jesus as her Savior. Mom and Dad wanted to see all their children trust Christ more than anything else.

The Accident

One afternoon at Camp Chetek, a counselor asked me about my interest in spiritual matters. I listened politely and answered his questions. But I'm not sure how serious I was since my mind was focused on the swimming time I was missing! After our conversation ended, swimming time was over. I recall the annoyance I felt while standing near the beach with less than five minutes left of swim time. Swimming with the other campers was more important to me than knowing Jesus Christ.

On our drive home from camp, six of us were in a car accident. Becky, a sophomore that fall, was thrown face first into the windshield and required fifty-two stitches. We all marveled at her recovery. Her constant smile still brings cheer to others wherever she goes. She turned a temporary tragedy into a positive view of life.

Mom suffered a concussion and Tom bruised his chest from hitting the steering wheel. I was hurt in the accident as well. Sitting in the back seat, long before seatbelts existed, I was thrown hard against the seat in front of me. The impact broke the thigh bone in my right leg. I remember John being alert and helping us all get out of the car.

I was in traction in the hospital for five weeks. Today, the recovery from a similar injury would be much less dramatic. During that time, my family gathered frequently at my bedside. But under the hospital's rules, John (13) and Dan (10) were too young to enter my room. Several times they visited me from outside my hospital room window. John remembers one of the nurses, the wife of the football and wrestling coach, let him and Dan into the hospital a number of times so they could visit me in my room.

John believes God used this time following my injury to give us a special bond as brothers. Seeing I needed extra help as I recovered, John was more helpful and caring for me than he had been. Our natural rivalry as brothers turned into a more caring attitude toward one another. I do think John missed all our brotherly rival-ries however, and was anxious to have me back in shape to compete with him.

Laid Up for a While

While I was recovering in the hospital, Dad did something I will never forget. He would take his noon lunch break from work at the Cumberland feed mill and eat with me in my room. He sat at the end of my bed, and we talked and ate together.

Today I have little memory of what we talked about, *but I will never forget him being there.* A few years later, when I was tempted to be a cynical, critical teenager who thought his dad uneducated and way behind the times, the relationship he and I developed during this time helped keep me from foolishly challenging him.

Our family proved we could stick together, not only in the good times but also in the difficult. Later this lesson proved to be valuable for John and me as we pursued our Olympic dreams. At various times when we were disappointed with losses and unfulfilled dreams, we always knew a family member would be ready to cheer us up and share the disappointment. Our family would encourage us repeatedly before sending us off to training camp, and they would join us at our competitions whenever possible.

After five weeks in the hospital, I finally got to go home. A big plaster cast, too heavy for me to lift, kept me in bed for another six weeks. For several months after that, I needed crutches. My leg had been broken, but God had not left me all alone. Rather, He was letting me heal, letting me feel His love, and letting me feel my family's love.

During this lengthy recovery, I had plenty of time to think. I recall thinking, "Since God is all-powerful, He could have kept me from the car accident." But He didn't. I also had time to rehearse the marker that had happened in John's life a full year before.

John's Marker

During the summer of 1961 when John was twelve, our family had taken a trip to the Minnesota State Fairgrounds to attend a Billy Graham Crusade. After the message, an invitation was given to anyone who wanted to trust Christ as their Savior. We were sitting close to the top of the grandstand; it was the highest thing I had ever been on.

All of a sudden, John got up and started walking down to the front. To me it looked like an awfully long ways. I thought, "What is John doing?! Why is he going with all those other people?" Then Dad stood up and followed John. I thought maybe Dad was going to bring him back; but no, they walked together all the way to the platform.

The following week, John received and completed a brief follow-up Bible Study Course. I recall John's diligence in doing the study and Mom and Dad's encouragement. By the next summer I saw John had a new perspective which attracted my attention.

Today, it is hard to imagine how that marker could be overemphasized. John was a new believer on a new course to honor God.

When I was twelve years old, I thought seriously about my personal relationship with God. I became interested in really knowing Him for myself. John had publicly declared his faith in Christ a year earlier and I began to see a real change in his confidence regarding important life matters. I wanted that same confidence for myself, but wasn't quite ready.

Today I consider my injury, and the time spent recovering from it, one of the most important times of my life. God knew I was thinking about Him. Yet until then, I had no real urgency about it. Growing up and having fun was my main focus. God allowed my leg to be broken so He could change my heart. The next summer at camp I chose to believe in Jesus, and I told other campers about my decision. My faith in Him has continued to grow ever since.

For a long time after the accident, I felt put aside and greatly limited. Certainly any thought of the Olympic Games never crossed my mind. In time, my healing was complete and I was running and playing again. Two years later, I entered Cumberland High School and began playing freshman football, and I began wrestling.

By that time, I had recovered from the accident with only a few lingering limitations. Occasionally I heard a teammate complain about the rigors of intense training, especially when we trained several times a day. But I would actually be looking forward to it. After being laid up for so long I was glad to be able to work hard again.

I'd been seriously injured and broken for a time, but I'd not been defeated or crushed by my injuries. **I found that with time, broken bones and even a broken spirit can heal.**

—4—
DABBLING AND DELAY

Full recovery from the car accident took time and real effort. When my cast finally came off, my leg was a weak and scrawny sight to see. But it looked great to me! It was finally ready to rehabilitate. John remembers watching me try to walk for the first time. It was painful for him to see the look of fear on my face as I began working my newly mended leg.

Rehabilitation meant exercising regularly with two beanbags Mom put together for me: a light one to start with, and a heavier one to use as my leg grew stronger. At age twelve, this was my first "leg extension machine." It was simple, and it worked. Sitting on the kitchen counter with the beanbag hanging over my foot, I extended my leg up, and then I let it down. I did this again and again, more than once a day. Before long, I did this same beanbag exercise with my healthy leg to keep it just as strong as the injured one.

Years later, when I would use professional leg machines, I would think of the beanbags and thank God for a wise doctor and a persistent mom. They got me lifting early!

Getting in the Game

After more than a year of healing, I could finally use my leg to run and play again. As an eighth grader, I tried junior high basketball. After practicing faithfully all season, I played for two minutes in the final quarter of the last game. Although I had plenty of height for my age, coordination was a real problem. I easily concluded that basketball was not the sport for me. That same school year, I experimented a little with wrestling, just as John had done the year before.

Coach Joe Hegenbarth was our junior high math teacher and had started the wrestling program at Cumberland High School. He had coached Tom and Phil, but was not coaching at the high school now. Later he would return to the high school as the varsity coach. He was extraordinarily successful as shown by his 1994 induction into the Wisconsin Wrestling Hall of Fame.

For two weeks, a wrestling mat was rolled out onto the stage of the junior high gymnasium. In physical education classes and after school, Coach Hegenbarth taught us wrestling. An intramural tournament was the culmination of those two weeks. I had one match in the tournament and won it. I rather liked wrestling!

John had two or three weeks of wrestling instruction from Coach Hegenbarth in his eighth grade P.E. class as well. A mini tournament followed and John lost in the finals to Dick Nelson. Dick kidded him years later about that loss. He was a good athlete and later played varsity basketball on the team that finished third in the 1965 Wisconsin State Basketball Tournament. John is not embarrassed at all to have lost to Dick. Dick also knows he could never win again.

Through watching Tom and Phil wrestle, learning basic instruction in eighth grade P.E., and our many spontaneous matches at home, we were gaining a steady familiarity with wrestling. John and I decided that when we got to high school we would wrestle.

John's Freshman Football Injury

John played freshman football when I was in eighth grade. He was strong, quick, and aggressive, but he weighed just 95 pounds. He was a running back and a defensive back. Being tackled by bigger teammates caused his body to take more of a beating than he was prepared to take. After one particularly hard tackle a few weeks into practice, his right knee was damaged enough to cause severe swelling. Our family doctor immediately drained the fluid off the knee and had him on crutches for the better part of two months. He developed a chronic case of "water on the knee," which the doctor would drain about every two weeks. Today, John believes this was an incorrect course of treatment. Had it been properly treated, he would have been back in a few weeks. John states our country has come a long way in treating sports injuries.

In November, when the high school wrestling season began, John's knee was still not well enough to start practice. And he sat out the entire year. He sometimes remarks he could have been the varsity 98-pounder as a freshman. This same knee would require surgery after his junior year to remove some cartilage.

Although it was a great disappointment for him not to compete in wrestling his entire freshman year, he realized that good things can come from bad situations. He learned the value of rest, ice, and rebuilding his muscle strength while recovering from his knee injury. During the time he was unable to wrestle, John also learned the importance of protecting himself against further injury. He would later nurse his body successfully through various ailments during many years of international wrestling.

You Won't Walk When You're Forty!

The knee became a nagging problem at the end of John's junior wrestling season. Every so often, a piece of cartilage would cause his knee to lock up. He would stop the action and with his right hand find and move the piece around until he could straighten out his leg again. As soon as the season was over, he had surgery to remove the piece of cartilage. This was before the days of orthoscopic surgery. Our two family doctors operated on the knee using only local anesthesia. John remembers the doctors having a difficult time finding the piece during surgery. His confidence waned when one doctor asked him if he could feel where the piece was. After a time of searching, they were successful in removing it.

When the knee swelled up during the first few weeks of the next football season, one of the surgery doctors told John if he continued to participate in football and wrestling he would not be able to walk when he was forty. He certainly proved that doctor wrong. To their credit, they did the best they could with the medical knowledge they had at the time.

Although the knee would continue to trouble him throughout his wrestling career, he had learned the importance of correct rehabilitation treatment. A second operation to remove more cartilage became necessary after the 1979 World Championships. By then, the surgery was much improved and he was back on the mat within a few weeks.

Lessons Learned from Our Dabbling and Delay

Looking back now, our low-key start in wrestling turned out to be a real benefit for us. We learned several key lessons that would help us later:

- When we finally got an opportunity to wrestle, we were eager for the hard training and pressure-filled competition wrestling provides.
- We learned we needed to protect ourselves against injury and wrestle safely. Years later, when we were among the heavier ones in the practice room, we trained with the biggest wrestlers around: the unlimited heavyweights. My college and Olympic teammate, Chris Taylor, was 6'5" and 425 pounds. To train with the heavyweights, we applied what we had learned in our early years of wrestling regarding avoiding injury. We learned that by carefully and systematically watching others as they trained and competed, we could learn a good amount of safe positioning.
- We also learned we could want something very badly without losing hope for earning it in the future. When injuries happened later, forcing us into a rest-ice-rehab approach, these were important lessons to have learned.

All this reminds me of the following words from Scripture: *"But those who wait on the Lord will renew their strength; they will mount up with wings like eagles, they will run and not be weary, they will walk and not faint." Isaiah 40:31*

In our earliest days in wrestling, when we were just dabbling in it and delayed by injuries, John and I learned to recognize when it was time to fly like an eagle, run like a sprinter, walk like a gentleman, or just sit the next one out.

Dad has his hands full at this picnic.

John in 4th grade, 3rd to the left from the teacher in the back row.
I am in 3rd grade and 3rd from the teacher in the middle row.

Childhood boxing.

The family go-cart with Dan at the controls and me, Phil, John, Tom, and Becky ready to push.

Above: New pups for the Petersons.

Right: Broken leg and crutches - 12 years old.

Above: Dan, John, and me playing with the calves.

Above: John and I found the beef - one of Dad's black angus.

Dad and Mom at our dining room table.

Left: Ben
7th grade.

Right: John
7th grade.

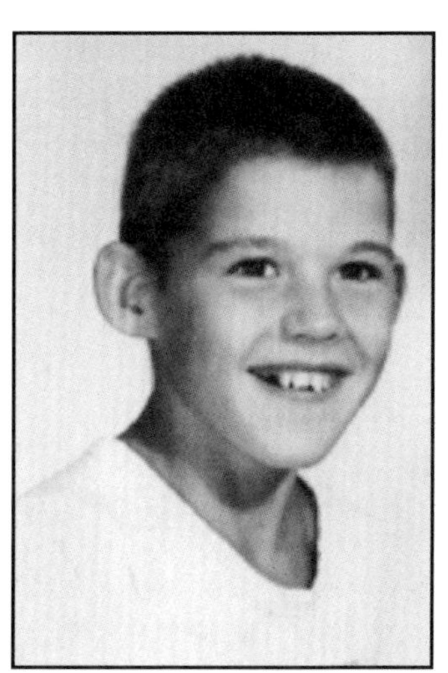

The Petersons all grown up - Phil, Tom, Becky, John, Ben, and Dan.

High School Sports

—5—
FINALLY, WE GET TO WRESTLE

Going into our first year of wrestling, John and I had almost no actual wrestling experience. Except for P.E. class, we had no grade school, no junior high, and no club wrestling programs available to us. Plus, John's knee injury kept him out of action for a full year. As we started wrestling in high school, it looked like we didn't have much going for us. It was a good thing we had hours of physical competition at home with our older brothers who were passing their knowledge along to us.

By this time, Mom was far more knowledgeable about wrestling and enthusiastic about the sport. We began high school wrestling with the full support of both parents. Our whole family was looking forward to the upcoming Cumberland High School wrestling season.

Our First Season

John and I weighed about 130 pounds each and we practiced together much of the time. We both hoped to make the junior varsity and get in some matches. As the season began, John earned the JV spot at 127. Although neither of us was ready for varsity competition, I hoped that John (a sophomore) would soon make the varsity so I could wrestle JV in his place. John started the season strong, winning his first three matches by pins against Turtle Lake, Unity, and Clear Lake.

As a freshman, I was having a growth spurt and my goal changed to wrestling JV at 133 pounds. About this time, our 133 pound varsity wrestler, who had been pinned in each match, decided he did not need to cut weight just to get pinned again. So John got a chance to wrestle varsity at 133. In that match, he got the first takedown but then gave up a flurry of points and was finally pinned. That same night I had my first JV match and won by a score of 3-1.

The Christmas holidays gave us a break from making weight for a couple weeks and I think I grew more. After break, I earned the 133 pound JV position and won by a forfeit to Ladysmith while John suffered his first JV loss 0-6 at 127. Interestingly, the opposing coach for Ladysmith, Jack Walsh, would apply at Cumberland to be the Biology teacher and the head football and wrestling coach for the next year. We had no idea of it at the time, nor did we know the tremendous impact he would eventually have on us.

I lost my next JV match 0-4, and John lost by a score of 0-5.

Our 133 and 138 pound varsity wrestlers were both having difficulty making weight. To give them a week off from this, John and I were on the varsity for one meet against our archrivals, the Chetek Bulldogs. Each of us was pinned in the first period. We were outclassed and Chetek beat our Cumberland Beavers that night 40-8. We did not know it then, but John wrestled a freshman named Harry Rhodes who would be a four-time state tournament qualifier and a state champion as a senior. The following year it would be my turn to wrestle Harry.

The week following our one-sided losses to Chetek, both of us were back on the JV team: this time against the Barron Bears. We each pinned our opponent and a week later, John pinned his wrestler from Spooner.

Making Varsity

About this time, I had a tryout match with our varsity 138-pounder. He was a senior and was tired of cutting weight just to lose most of the time. I do not think he was very motivated that night. At the end of our wrestle-off, I was ahead by one point and had earned a spot on our struggling varsity team.

The same night I won that match, a fellow freshman wrestler rolled over my left hand and dislocated my ring finger. The injury exposed the root of my fingernail, causing infection under it. Mom sent me to the doctor. His orders were simple: soak my finger in hot water several times a day, and *no more wrestling for three weeks.* With that, I knew my wrestling season was over. The regional tournament was two and a half weeks away. I'd already missed practice to go to the doctor, so I was a little worried walking back to school to tell Coach Rutter about my doctor visit.

Coach Rutter surprised me when he said he wanted me to keep wrestling. When I told him what the doctor had said, he replied, "A little infection in a finger shouldn't stop a man from doing his work. I'll get a metal protector for your finger, and you get your parent's permission to keep on wrestling." Mom and Dad said, "Yes, you can wrestle." I think Dad reasoned, "No infected finger would keep a dairy farmer from milking cows, nor should it stop his son from doing his sport."

Before I wrestled my first varsity match though, Coach Rutter thought it best for me to sit out our meet the next evening with Spooner. During this time, my coaches and teammates worked a little extra with me to get me ready to wrestle varsity. A problem for me was my swollen left hand did not allow me to hold my opponent's left elbow when starting on top in the referee's position. My coaches and teammates taught me to start from the opposite side of my opponent so I could use my uninjured right hand instead. As a result, I was equally comfortable in the referee's position on either side of an opponent from that time on. Many wrestlers never develop this skill. Again, something good came out of something initially bad.

Everyone knew John was the better wrestler between the two of us, so he asked Coach Rutter for a tryout for my varsity spot at 138. Coach told John he would need to beat everyone else in the weight class before he could wrestle me. John would have to "wrestle up the ladder;" that is, he would need to beat the former varsity wrestler I had defeated before he could challenge me. John lost and was unable to challenge me. I guess the other guy was determined to save face and not let two brothers beat him in the same week!

That weekend, we competed in an invitational tournament. I was pinned twice and put out of the tournament. The next week, we faced Grantsburg in a dual meet. I was pinned in 2:20 while John got a pin on JV. Coach Rutter still hadn't found a winning 138 pound wrestler for our team, yet he insisted I had the varsity spot at that weight.

In our Heart O' North Conference Tournament the results were the same: two more losses by pins. The next week in the regional tournament, which is the first step to the WIAA Individual State Wrestling Tournament, I was pinned again. Mercifully, this ended my first wrestling season.

My freshman JV record was four wins and one loss. But on varsity, my record was no wins and seven losses; and all seven varsity losses were by pins.

Sometimes I tell wrestlers I started out with a perfect record with all pins. But I would have given anything to stay off my back in those seven matches!

I also tell people I really lost fourteen times on varsity that year. I lost every match and also lost every attempt to avoid being pinned and giving my opponent's team extra points.

Our Hope for the Future

The main thing I remember about our first season was the people around us were so positive about our wrestling. Although I lost every varsity match by a pin, people were still hopeful about my wrestling future. This gave me confidence as I looked forward to the next season. I did not really have the sense of discouragement that a 0-7 record would imply.

After getting so much positive support from others, John and I were more determined to do our best the next year. With our parents providing us a positive, God-honoring perspective at home, our church teaching us important truths from God's Word, and our teammates, coaches, family, and friends all encouraging us to do better the next year, we could hardly wait for the next wrestling season to begin.

Young wrestlers need hope for the future. Hope keeps them going strong while they dream of future success, train hard to get better, and compete. Family, friends, teammates, coaches, teachers, and fans can be so helpful when they see even a hint of potential in a young athlete and communicate a positive attitude to that young person. This encouragement from others sparked a flame that burned in John and me all the way to the Olympic Games.

—6—

BUILDING CONFIDENCE: OUR SECOND YEAR

After we finished our first wrestling season, we learned that Coach Rutter was leaving to lead a Minnesota community college football program as its first head coach. Coach Rutter knew little about wrestling except that it was good for his football players. His main interest was football. With Coach Rutter leaving Cumberland, we wondered about our future in athletics.

Soon it was announced that Jack Walsh was coming to Cumberland as our new head football and head wrestling coach. I remember some apprehension, and maybe even some distrust, regarding Coach Walsh. He was coming to us from nearby Ladysmith High School: one of our biggest wrestling and football rivals in our conference. Coach Walsh was a Chicago native with a good background in wrestling and coaching. He was also hired to teach high school biology.

Confidence in Our New Coach

Before we ever met Coach Walsh, we each got a nice letter from him urging us to train hard over the summer and to be fully prepared and conditioned to compete in the fall.

Just before football practice, we got to know Coach Walsh by helping him move his family into the temporary home they were renting in Cumberland. Later, we helped them move into a more permanent home. John and I, along with our teammates, were getting to know our new coach who would really teach us how to wrestle. We came to understand that Coach cared deeply about each of us, both as students and as athletes. He was willing and able to help us set our wrestling goals and guide us toward reaching them.

Confidence in Our Strength and Conditioning

That summer, Phil was home from the University of Wisconsin. He promptly went to work with the barbells training for Big Ten football. John immediately began lifting weights with him. Their pace was more demanding than I wanted, so I often stayed away from their basement weight room. Later, I realized Phil was teaching us to move beyond our competition by using weightlifting as a key part of our off-season training. It would be another two years before I took weight training as seriously as John and Phil.

Confidence in Sound Wrestling Technique

John remembers something new that year - technique charts! Coach Walsh posted a number of them in our practice room. Wrestling moves were shown in pictures, step-by-step, so we could all study the progression of a move from its beginning to its end. This was the first time we had seen moves broken down into separate steps. We were then expected to drill through several of those moves each day. John was more faithful in doing this than I was, but it taught us a lot of sound positioning. Later, when we saw entire books of wrestling techniques set out in progression, we absorbed them like sponges.

Today I can still recall many of the moves Coach Walsh first taught us using these technique charts. A turk leg-hook working into a pin was useful all the way to the Olympics. We were also taught the following pinning combinations: nelsons, cradles, and arm-bars. The Cornell drop (used to finish a single-leg takedown), double-leg takedowns, a whizzer, the Navy ride, switches and stand-ups, a deep-waist ride, and the far-ankle ride were each systematically taught to us by Coach Walsh.

Many of these moves are the building blocks of great wrestling at any level, and we used them throughout our wrestling years, including in the Olympic Games. We still teach them to others at our summer wrestling camps.

However, for both John and me, the most important move of all was the double-leg takedown. We kept refining it and building options off of it right on through high school, into college, and during our years in international competition. John mastered the double-leg takedown in every way. Today, he is an expert teacher of the double-leg. From the beginning, Coach Walsh gave us full confidence in the double-leg takedown.

Coach taught us to climb the exercise rope he had installed in the corner of our high school gym. He taught us sound wrestling technique, but he also emphasized the strength we needed to complete the wrestling moves we were drilling in practice. Climbing the exercise rope helped give us the strength we needed to wrestle well.

At Christmas break, John, who was now a junior, had a varsity record of four wins (three by pins) and no losses. As a sophomore, my record at break was two wins and one loss.

Confidence Learned from Others

At the end of Christmas break Coach Walsh set up a scrimmage with a neighboring school. Turtle Lake was smaller than Cumberland and in a conference that played eight-man football. I am sure Coach was trying to expand our experience and build our confidence.

Some of us found we were able to defeat our opponents in most situations. In scrimmages, all areas of the sport can be worked on repeatedly. Just working with someone new is refreshing, and John and I felt good about our success. It is always good to win!

But our teammates in the upper middle weights were shaking their heads in disbelief. Their opponents had gotten the best of them in every position. They talked of one wrestler by the name of Gary Sorum who "wrestled in series." He kept moving from one position to the other, constantly adjusting to create another opportunity to improve his position and defeat his opponents. They described a way of wrestling that was aggressive, continual, exciting to watch, and very hard to stop. My teammate's comments sparked my interest; I wanted to see and know how to compete that way.

The question arose in my mind, "What does it mean to wrestle in series?" We did not see that team again until we attended the regionals, where all athletes started their quest for state qualification. The Turtle Lake team was there and I looked forward to seeing "series wrestling." I wanted to watch Sorum and see what that meant and why it beat my teammates so badly.

As I rested between matches in the locker room, a coach and a team member carried a wrestler in. The coach laid him down on a training table and began giving instructions for getting him some water and a candy bar while he mumbled, "He shouldn't even have wrestled. He is too sick to wrestle again." At the time, I did not know who the sick wrestler was. On the way home it was made clear that he was the "series wrestler," the guy we all wanted to watch.

We returned for the second day of competition hoping Gary Sorum would be there. He was not. He was too sick to come to weigh-ins. It was disappointing not to see the man who was a four time conference champion and a contender for state-level wrestling. The exciting "always moving" style could not overcome illness. This ended Gary's senior year and he never wrestled again.

I was learning that many factors can affect a wrestler's success. Taking care of the body's health and asking for God's protection and blessing is essential.

Confidence Built Through Improved Competition

Another key memory for me from that season was our reaction when Coach Walsh scheduled two dual meets with Superior High School. We all knew that Superior's student enrollment was three times larger than ours, and some of our upperclassmen questioned the wisdom of placing Superior on our schedule. But Coach insisted that we were ready, and told us that taking them on was a way for us to gain confidence in ourselves.

For some reason, I was not in the lineup that night. But I remember traveling with our team on the bus two hours north to Superior. They had a new school building with classrooms on each side of a main circular hallway. The school seemed massive to us and we decided to walk around it. Halfway around, we feared we might be late for the meet and we quickened our pace.

That evening, we won all but one of our varsity matches and we returned to Cumberland feeling terrific! Coach Walsh told everyone about our big win. The names and telephone numbers of area radio and television stations are still written in the front of our team scorebook from that year. Coach Walsh made sure they all knew about our *David vs. Goliath* victory.

In February, we wrestled Superior again: this time in Cumberland. For a second time, we won convincingly 38-6. Never again would we fear a wrestling team or an individual wrestler just because they came from a bigger school.

Coach Walsh started the Cumberland Invitational Tournament that year. Wrestling on our old horsehair mat, and on our new *Resilite®* mat, made the tournament memorable for us. But winning the tournament made the biggest impression. Coach Walsh really knew what he was doing in scheduling our wrestling meets: he was building our team's confidence.

John finished the dual-meet portion of our season that year with ten wins and just one loss, and he had seven pins. My dual-meet record was six wins, three losses, and one tie. I had six pins. Harry Rhodes from Chetek pinned me. As I've mentioned earlier, Harry would be a Wisconsin state champion two years later.

Except for Harry pinning me, I had definitely improved from the previous year when I had no wins and seven losses by pin. Our overall team record that season was nine wins and two losses. In the end, our self-confidence soared with Coach Walsh as our leader.

As we concluded our second year of wrestling, John and I learned from Coach that there was much, much more about wrestling we did not know. We could continue to improve and get better. And our wrestling competitions showed that we were making real progress.

We also learned our wrestling season was not really over with the end of the high school schedule. In the off-season, we switched to weightlifting and conditioning as part of our training. To continue improving and to reach our full wrestling potential, we needed to train hard in the off-season. We needed to improve our strength and become better conditioned. John determined to lift weights with Phil for another summer. I followed them in the weight room too, but only when convenient.

As we trained together that summer, we often talked about wrestling and football. It was easier to talk about wrestling that summer than it had been before. Thanks to Coach Walsh's expert coaching, we now had actual names and descriptions for our wrestling moves and could talk more precisely about our sport.

—7—

SERIOUS ATHLETIC PREPARATION

Phil built a real weight room in the basement of our house. This is where John and I changed from being two country boys casually playing children's games into two men working hard and smart to excel at our sports: wrestling and football.

My first recollection of Phil lifting weights was pretty crude. He had managed to find a long pipe, and had attached the wheel rims from an old abandoned car to the ends of the pipe for weights. With this heavy homemade concoction, he did overhead presses, curls, and deadlifts.

I ran into him on my way through the basement one day and asked, "What are you doing?"

He answered, "The university football players lift weights and I want to be ready."

A thirteen year old and an eighteen year old can communicate really well or not much at all. That day it was not much at all. I would stay and watch once in a while, but not that day.

Phil started with a small BUR barbell set. A year or so later, he bought a larger York barbell set. Still later he bought additional York barbell plates as he gained strength.

We made our own bench for bench presses. It was built from old wood we covered with vinyl, and we filled the vinyl with stuffing taken from the back seat of the old abandoned car. Our bench had two wooden brackets to hold the bar between lifts, and it had two other lower brackets to catch the barbell if we lifted alone and couldn't quite finish a lift. We also made our own lat pulldown machine using old barn-cleaner pulleys. And we made an isometric rack and a full squat rack out of wood. We used this weight room equipment for many years.

By today's standards, our basement model was makeshift at

best. But we put together this weight room well before any area high schools had organized weight training for their athletes. Primitive though it was, in the 1960s and early '70s we may have had one of the best weight rooms in all of northern Wisconsin. Regardless, it worked great for us and gave us added confidence and a real edge over our competition.

Phil and John were always looking for ways to improve as athletes, and John and I greatly benefitted from the knowledge Phil brought home from the university. All of this was at a time before weight training had widely caught on as an effective way to train and condition athletes. We heard many coaches cautioning athletes to stay away from heavy barbells because, "You could injure yourself or become too muscle bound for your sport."

From 1963-1966, Phil had a Wisconsin football teammate who was way ahead of his time using the weight room to train athletes. Kim Wood became a good lifting mate for Phil. He was a serious proponent of weight training for athletes in every sport. In 1963, Wood finished second in the Illinois State Wrestling Tournament at heavyweight for Barrington High School. In addition to football, Wood had a particular interest in weight training for wrestlers. He convinced Phil to buy and read the magazines *Strength & Health and Muscular Development,* published by Bob Hoffman of the York Barbell Company. Kim and Phil would read those magazines and talk about what they had read: the theory of strength training for athletes and how to put that theory into practice in the weight room.

This reading and discussion gave Phil the latest ideas on weight training. In particular, it gave him the idea of overload training which enables an athlete to become stronger and stronger by regularly going to the maximum he can lift. Phil drew on these same ideas as he equipped our weight room in the basement, and then we used those ideas during our weight training exercises.

Kim Wood proved to be an authentic, lasting authority on weight training for athletes. His life's work for twenty-eight years was to serve as the full-time strength and conditioning coach for the Cincinnati Bengals of the National Football League. Kim was one of the first full-time strength coaches in all of American sports. Without knowing it, we were being exposed to lifting ideas that are common knowledge in most lifting rooms today. I knew very little about the philosophy behind the lifting, I just knew I was getting stronger when I regularly lifted Phil's way.

Lesson learned: regularly working hard with crude apparatus is better than doing nothing while longing and waiting for more up-to-date equipment.

—8—

TWO STEPS FORWARD, ONE STEP BACK

In the spring of my sophomore year and John's junior year, we began preparing for our next wrestling season. Neither John nor I played baseball or ran track in the spring, so we began our off-season training by working out after school three times a week in our basement weight room. This kept us both hard at work all spring.

Summer Training

Phil came home in June for the summer and added some intensity to our training. John eagerly accepted the challenge with new maturity and focus. And Dan, going into eighth grade in the fall, often joined us.

To John and Phil, lifting weights, running for conditioning, and hitting our homemade football blocking sled were a priority. They missed very few training sessions all summer long. Hard summer training would give them an edge during their competitive seasons.

As we trained together, Phil talked about playing offensive guard in the fall for the Badgers and graduating the next spring from the university. He planned to serve in the Army (the Vietnam War draft required it), and afterwards attend law school. He was identifying and developing his goals and was motivated to work hard to reach them. John spoke about playing guard and linebacker on the football team, winning a state wrestling championship at 154 pounds, graduating from high school, and attending college the following year.

Phil encouraged and guided John in his academic and athletic goals. Mom and Dad watched while voicing their approval. I was somewhat helped by this goal-setting talk, but I was not yet mature enough to focus on it fully. It would be another year before that would happen.

Football

Phil left for college in late August and John and I played together on the football team. As a senior co-captain, John developed his leadership skills by leading other players in extra training. Even so, our team's record that fall was poor with just one win and seven losses.

In two games, while playing both offensive guard and linebacker, John demonstrated his fearless determination to compete. He suffered a concussion and couldn't remember the football plays. He kept asking our teammates what he should do on each play. He even asked the other players not to tell Coach because John knew he would take him out of the game.

In the second game where this happened, John took himself out after he was confused about who to defend in passing situations. Although this type of foolhardy courage is certainly not recommended for anyone, it showed John had fierce competitive determination.

My football season that year was nothing special. On offense and defense, I played as an end and caught only three passes all season. I once caught a pass for an extra point only to have the play called back because the referees thought I was an ineligible receiver downfield. I had been playing tight end on offense for the entire game, and since I was normally a blocking tight end, the referees mistakenly thought I was an ineligible receiver. This call came against our archrival, the Rice Lake Warriors. John, as our co-captain and perhaps as my older brother, forcefully but unsuccessfully pleaded our case to an official.

Glen Cunningham

During this school year an assembly was held for all students. The speaker was an older man but we have never forgotten the story he told.

While attending a small country school in Kansas, Glen Cunningham was involved in a fire that took the life of his older brother and burned Glen's legs to the point he could not feel or move them. The doctors were not optimistic and suggested amputation and walking on artificial legs. Glen pleaded to keep his legs, and his father agreed. They massaged his limp legs by the hour while talking and praying together until the circulation and nerves began to function again. Day after day, out of sheer determination, Glen pulled himself up using the back door railing and stumbled to walk. After repeatedly falling and trying again, he was able to stumble into a staggering walk.

Eventually, he was able to run. Running wherever he went, Glen gained his neighbors' encouragement, "Run, boy, run!" While competing in a race at the county fair, he told of his prayer which has often encouraged me: "Lord, if you will pick up my legs, I will put them down. But I will not quit!"

Glen went on to become a national and international running hero and won a silver medal in the 1936 Olympic Games in Berlin.

Leaving the assembly that day, I wondered how far I could go if I used the same determination Glen possessed. What could I do as a student and as an athlete if I would not quit in preparation and competition?

Glen Cunningham has been a calm but repeated reminder, "Don't quit, Ben. Don't quit!"

Wrestling Season

The season began with renewed optimism. Our winning dual-meet record the previous season, combined with many returning starters in our lineup, led Coach Walsh and John, as team captain, to look for extra training possibilities to stretch us to new heights. We ran laps around the gym before practice and sprints after practice in the long hallway to improve our conditioning.

We ran pre-practice laps around the outer edge of the basketball court while the basketball players did their pre-practice shooting. The basketball coach did not like us running there, especially since we would occasionally stop, pick up a stray basketball, and take a shot of our own. This created some tension between the wrestlers and the basketball team.

One day while running laps, John grabbed a basketball and took a shot. (I think he made it!) John had taken the basketball away from Jim, one of my friends and a classmate. Jim was not happy with John grabbing the basketball, and he went after John as a street fighter might do. John immediately tossed him in a wrestling move.

The next day John apologized to Jim, but I told Jim that attacking John as he had was not very smart. Maybe my friend Jim really did win. After that, we wrestlers left the bouncing basketballs alone, and as we ran by, we talked a bit more respectfully to the basketball players.

John started sprinting regularly in the school hallway after practice and he invited the rest of us to join him. At first we resisted the idea, but when we saw the value in better conditioning and in more wins, several of us joined him. This started what became my regular approach to conditioning: train hard and finish in a flurry. It is a valuable approach to conditioning that I used throughout my sixteen years of wrestling competition. I have coached many others to do the same sprinting workouts.

John showed two characteristics of strong leadership: train extra hard on your own and urge others to join you.

Both of us improved significantly. Wrestling at 154 pounds, John had thirteen wins (with five pins) and just one loss in our dual meets. He also won the Cumberland Invitational Tournament, Heart O' North Conference Tournament, and the regional tournament.

Wrestling at 165 pounds, my dual meet record was twelve wins (with six pins) and two losses. John kiddingly tells me heavier wrestlers are a lot easier to pin. Like John, I won the Cumberland Invitational Tournament, Heart O' North Conference Tournament, and the regional tournament.

This wrestling success was a big step forward for both of us. Our team finished the dual meet season with a record of nine wins and five losses.

John Stumbles

Our competition was much tougher when we got to the sectional tournament. Wisconsin has long had two qualifying tournaments leading up to its state tournament. First, every Wisconsin high school may enter one wrestler per weight class in the regional tournament. The top two advanced to the sectional tournament. Then those who placed first and second in a sectional qualified for the state tournament the following week.

After winning the regionals and winning in the early rounds of the sectional, we both lost in the semifinals. Although John's goal was a state championship, he lost 4-2 in the semis to Arlen Hansen of New Richmond. After losing to Hansen, John could still come back and qualify for state if he won his wrestleback matches and took second place. John won his first wrestleback match, enabling him to wrestle Edgell of Unity for true second place. John had beaten Edgell 4-0 earlier in the season. This time however, John stumbled and lost by a single point. He finished third in the sectional and did not qualify for the state tournament. The following week, Arlen Hansen won the state tournament at 154 pounds. John learned a bitter lesson — *an earlier win, even an easy one, does not count for much later when the stakes are much higher.* John had placed too much emphasis on winning a state championship and not enough on wrestling his best in every match along the way. John was stunned by his two losses in the sectional tournament and was particularly startled by his failure to qualify for state. For quite a few months afterward, John questioned whether he should even try out for the wrestling team in college.

Incidentally, thirty-three years later in 2000, John's middle son Josh, was in the same situation as John had been. Josh also lost in the sectional semifinals. But John got to watch him fight back from that loss, take second place in the sectional, and move on to the state tournament. Josh learned from his dad's experience. In the state finals a week later, Josh defeated the same wrestler who had beaten him the week before in the sectional. It was one short week for Josh between barely making it into the tournament to winning the state championship.

My Narrow Sectional Win

Part of training hard is pushing your body through certain limits while learning which limits the body is not designed to push through. It is a game in itself: figuring out when to override your body's feedback and when to honor it and give it time to re-balance before pressing on.

As John narrowly lost his second wrestleback match, I narrowly won mine. The score was tied coming down to the last seconds when I escaped using a standup, giving me the win and a second place finish. During those final seconds, I felt lightheaded and dizzy. In my dizziness, the gym wall, just 15 or so feet away, looked like it was moving back and forth. I settled down into a low stance and waited a moment for stability to return. Then I completed the stand-up for an escape and a win. I had qualified for the state tournament!

I learned a valuable lesson in that match. Whenever I have been lightheaded or dizzy from flurrying in practice or during a match, I have tried to stabilize myself first before moving on. I have seen others who were lightheaded or dizzy simply charge on and usually lose control.

State Wrestling Tournament

I have often said that during his junior and senior years, John showed me how to train for top-notch wrestling competition. Although he himself fell short of qualifying, John led me to state. And because John did not go, I felt alone: like I was limping along with something important missing. John tried to be positive and get me ready to compete at my best, but I could tell he was hurting badly inside. He was greatly disappointed he was not wrestling there as well.

John was really happy for me in spite of his disappointment. He was delighted that I had qualified for the state tournament. From matside at state, he encouraged me as I competed. I wrestled two matches and was pinned in both of them. One of my losses was to Rich Hinebaugh of Monroe, who went on to finish second. The following year, I would face Rich again.

Both of my opponents wore me down considerably. When this happened, they turned me over for the pin. The state tournament showed me a higher level of wrestling. I simply was not prepared for the constant barrage of moves, one right after the other I faced at this higher level.

Lessons

Later I would clearly remember the helpless feeling I felt as a junior in the state tournament. My memory of that helplessness would motivate me to; lift weights and get stronger, run and condition myself to be more fit, and drill and wrestle hard to polish my technique. I did all this so I would be ready to compete as a senior against wrestlers like those I had faced at state as a junior. My opponents were clearly a step or more ahead of me. I had seen what I needed to do to compete at that higher level and I was determined to be ready next time.

John and I learned many lessons that year. We greatly improved our strength, conditioning and technique, and we gained confidence. But it was not enough to match up against the competition we had faced at the end of the season. Winning a tight, tough wrestling match is never easy. It is always hard and never automatic.

We discovered losing was not fun. After a long year of hard training to reach our goal of winning the state tournament, losing was devastating. After his two losses in the sectional, John struggled with whether it was worthwhile for him to wrestle in college. He was a senior and would not return to high school wrestling in the fall. His motivation to train was greatly diminished and he was straining to find new hope.

After thinking long and hard about what my goals were as an athlete, and two weeks of rest following the state tournament, I was back in our basement weight room. I lifted weights with new purpose, preparing for next year's football season and a run at a state wrestling championship! I had one more year of high school left to see what I could do with the athletic talent God had given me. And I knew the only way to find that out was to train hard and apply the lessons I had learned.

John and I learned one thing for sure that season: two steps forward and one step back is far better than no steps forward at all.

—9—

KEEPING HOPE ALIVE

After the wrestling season ended his senior year, John struggled much of the spring and summer and questioned the value of trying to play a college sport. Unlike how he had trained the previous two summers, he now lacked the motivation to lift weights or to run much at all.

He would often say to me, "Ben, there's no reason for me to try college football. I'm just too small. And there's no sense in me trying to wrestle in college since I didn't even qualify for the state tournament." Instead of continuing with the off-season strength and conditioning training he had done in the past, his main focus now was on graduating from high school and earning money over the summer to help pay his upcoming college expenses.

One of John's most disheartening memories from the summer after he graduated was standing on the back steps of our house watching me get into the car of the wrestling coach from River Falls. The coach was running a wrestling camp not far from our home and I was on my way to that camp. As John watched, he was sad to think his wrestling days now seemed over and that he had not yet done what he had hoped to do in wrestling. Truly, John needed time to heal emotionally and renew his hope.

John Moves Beyond His Disappointment

One day that summer, Coach Walsh drove with John and me to Coon Rapids, Minnesota, to see a Greco-Roman wrestling tournament. U.S. Greco-Roman Coach Alan Rice organized the tournament as the Greco tryouts for the 1967 U.S. Pan American Team competing in Winnipeg, Canada. Although the Greco-Roman wrestling style was unfamiliar to us, the tournament was memorable. We were confused when the referees kept putting the wrestlers back up on their feet whenever there was too little action down on the mat. John kind of liked that idea because he thought he was a better wrestler on his feet than he was on the mat.

The Greco-Roman technique we saw in Coon Rapids amazed us. We could scarcely believe the wrestler's skill, timing, strength, and intensity. I have never forgotten it. It was an enormous eye opener about the level of competition wrestling can provide. Our trip to that tournament was particularly important for John since he needed encouragement to regain his enthusiasm for wrestling.

That fall, John enrolled as a freshman at the University of Wisconsin Stout (then called Stout State University.) Stout is located in Menomonie, about fifty miles south of our home. John enrolled with little intention of wrestling. But sometime that fall, at the urging of Phil, John talked with Coach Pierce about joining the team. John was surprised to learn that any Stout student could try out for the team. Later he was stunned when he won a starting spot on the varsity as a freshman. During the season, John placed third in the 1968 Wisconsin State University Conference Tournament. His freshmen season really excited him. Maybe he could be a college success, and maybe he had short-changed himself. He came home ready to lift and run to make his sophomore season even better.

Summer Training

Although I ended my junior season by losing badly at the state tournament, that season gave me a huge lift. By following in John's footsteps I developed a competitive intensity and a love for wrestling that has stayed with me ever since.

Just when I needed another boost in my training, Phil was there to help me. Four years earlier, after just two years of high school wrestling, Phil had qualified for the state tournament as a senior. As I began looking toward my senior year, Phil had just graduated from the University of Wisconsin. Following his senior football season, he was named to the first-team All Big Ten Academic Football Team. Phil assured me if I trained hard all spring and summer, I would have a good chance to win the state championship at 180 pounds and have a shot at a college scholarship. As an impressionable high school senior, his words meant a lot.

During the previous three summers, John and Phil's daily training intensity had seemed too much for me. But now I welcomed it. My hopes were high, and it made perfect sense to follow John and Phil's lifting and running routines. Although Phil had bought all our weights and had made our bench for bench presses, I took ownership of our weight room for myself. Instead of it being "Phil's" weight room, it was now "our" weight room. And indeed, now it really became "my" weight room.

When Phil arrived home from Madison in June, I expected him to continue his previous weight training and conditioning routines. I was excited to join him. But I was disappointed to learn that Phil had a new interest: law school! Studying for the Law School Admissions Test (LSAT) began in earnest for him that summer. With John too disheartened to keep training anymore, and with Phil always lost somewhere in all his law books, I was left to motivate myself. It was a valuable test of my own personal resolve to train alone, day after day, in the off-season.

It would have been much easier for me had I joined them the previous summer and learned how to train hard by following their examples. I remember scolding myself for my immaturity and lack of commitment. But all of that had long since passed, and the question for me was, "What will I do now?"

I had a full summer ahead of me to gain strength, improve my conditioning, develop a measure of maturity, and work hard to reach my wrestling and football goals. I decided to keep training hard and keep my hopes alive.

Mom also had valuable thoughts about my summer training that encouraged me and she talked to Phil and me about them. It was the spring and summer of 1967, during the Vietnam War, and Phil was about to be drafted into the Army. He would not need to report for three, or maybe even four months. Mom suggested Phil might be willing to help me train even though he was not training the same way himself.

Mom's idea convinced us, and Phil joined me in the basement to guide my weight training. I lifted three days a week and hit the wooden blocking sled in the backyard twice a week, along with other football drills. At that time I was also focused on the possibility of playing college football somewhere.

I worked at the vegetable canning factory in Cumberland. My

start time was 11:00 a.m. on most days, so I needed to complete my morning training before then. However, Phil's routine was to read his law books well into the night when it was quiet, and sleep late in the morning. Changing his routine caused some tension at first. Phil did not welcome my early morning wake-up calls. But he got up every morning and met me. He came to my workouts day after day, sometimes a little grumpy at first, but always with enthusiasm and encouragement for me before we finished.

During the Vietnam War, full-time college students had a draft deferment until they graduated. After Phil's college graduation in June, we expected he would soon be ordered to report to the Army. Throughout the summer we waited. It was not until late summer he received his orders to report in late September. I am so glad Uncle Sam delayed his call! This allowed Phil to personally guide me in one of the most intense summer training programs I ever participated in during my sixteen years as a competitor.

Flame of Hope

To stay at a difficult task for any length of time, hope must be regained after a setback, disappointment, or failure. When he could not see a future for himself in wrestling, John lost his motivation to train hard. In contrast, after I qualified as a junior for the state tournament, my hope for the future was greater than ever. Phil's daily encouragement in my summer training program set me on fire, and his guidance kept the flame hot.

If we lose hope, or if hope is delayed, we may face severe setbacks. In the words of Scripture: *"Hope deferred makes the heart sick, but when the desire comes it is a tree of life." Proverbs 13:12* When we lose hope, we lose energy and focus. But when hope is alive, we can accomplish great things through a focused significant effort. Hope for the future and confidence in our preparation are necessary to fully commit ourselves to any demanding task.

—10—
HOPE DEFERRED BUT STILL ALIVE!

Hope for the future gives us stability, steadiness, and consistency. It keeps us on course and gives us energy day after day. If we lose hope, or if hope is deferred (set aside or long in coming), we get discouraged. But if we do all, or even some, of what we hope for, we have new energy and a new excitement in life. As a high school senior I experienced all this, both the good and the bad.

Football Hopes

The fall of my senior year began with great hopes for a successful football season and maybe even for an opportunity to play college football. We had a new head coach, Bucky DiSalvo. Coach DiSalvo was a native of Cumberland and eager to come back as vice principal and head football coach. He returned from River Falls, a much larger high school in the area, where he had built an excellent record as their football coach.

I was playing a new position (for me) as a tackle on both offense and defense. Going into the season, I had a lot of confidence after being coached over the summer by Phil. At Wisconsin, Phil had been coached by their new offensive line coach, Mike McGee. While a student at Duke University, Coach McGee won the Outland Trophy which was awarded each year to the best college football interior lineman in the country. He also played three years in the NFL for the St. Louis Cardinals. He taught Phil a lot of sound technique that Phil taught to me. As a result, my hopes for the new football season were high.

Our first four games were all hard fought, but we came up short in each of them. Our team was playing hard, and we were improving. But our hope was delayed.

The next three games were just ugly. After trying to start with some excitement and confidence, our team folded in each game. We finished our conference schedule with a record of no wins and seven losses and last in the Heart O' North Conference.

This left our team with one non-conference football game to end our season, one last chance for us to gain some self-respect. Throughout the game, both individually and as a team, we went from hope to despair, back and forth several times. It was a wide-open, high-scoring game. Our other defensive tackle, Brian Kamnetz, and I sacked our opponent's quarterback repeatedly. A teacher at school complimented me the next week by saying my number "74" must be permanently sealed on the opposing quarterback's chest. But for all our sacks, I still remember too often getting up after the play only to see that a pass had been completed against us somewhere downfield. Sadly, in our final game of the season, we lost again.

As I look back on that season of football and how hard I worked to be an effective player, I lacked one key element: training with my teammates. Yes, I was learning and getting stronger, but I was not doing much as a team leader. I had little, if any, contact with the rest of the players in town during the summer when I was making my own personal progress.

Today, my son, who has coached football and specializes in strength and explosive training, says that even mediocre workout programs can help a team that works out together more than a brilliant workout plan done by a bunch of separated individuals. An indescribable strength develops within a group that trains and has fun together.

In a few more years, Coach DiSalvo would go on to coach a number of fine winning football teams in Cumberland. Our younger brother, Dan, played on three of those teams. But for us in 1967, all our football hope was denied: we ended our season with no wins. Personally, my dream of playing college football slowly faded away until it was gone.

Looking back, I see I needed to give up football dreams to make room for bigger things coming my way in wrestling. As it turned out, God had given me much more talent in wrestling than in football.

Wrestling Hopes

My senior wrestling season began just three days after the last of our disheartening football losses. The excitement of a new wrestling season, with its clean slate, gave us new hope. Instead of losing everything, we began winning almost everything Coach Walsh scheduled for us.

By midseason, we were ranked in the "Sweet 16" of Wisconsin high school wrestling teams. Wrestling at 180 pounds, I won every match. Dan made the varsity as a freshman forcing another senior and good friend of mine to cut weight. Jim's great attitude about cutting weight made our team even stronger. Our hopes were high again for another good wrestling season.

The season was going great for us until the unimaginable happened. While wrestling in practice with Coach, I did a standing roll against him, blocking his ankle on the way down. As a result, my roll broke his ankle.

Of course Coach Walsh kidded me about it, as did everyone else. In the end, though, something positive came out of this accident. A picture of Coach in his walking cast alongside "the wrestler who broke his coach's leg" made it all the way onto the front page of the national wrestling magazine, *Amateur Wrestling News.* This gave our little school some good recognition. While none of us would have made that trade, something positive emerged to make it more bearable.

My undefeated record raised my hopes of qualifying for the state tournament again. But coming from northwestern Wisconsin where we had little competition against the rest of the state during the regular season, gave me some worries about my readiness to compete against opponents from the big city schools or from the "big-time" schools around Wisconsin.

Since I had these doubts, even a casual comment from others could either help or hurt the development of my hopes over many months of serious training. I've never forgotten an encouraging comment from Harry Rhodes who was an outstanding wrestler from our conference archrival Chetek. At the regional tournament that year, Harry told me, "Ben, you can win the state tournament. The other wrestlers down there are no different than we are. I've made some mistakes, but I've also learned a lot from them. And I know I can win the state tournament, and so can you!" Just two weeks later, Harry won the Wisconsin State High School Wrestling Tournament. His comments stayed with me as I wrestled my way through the qualifying tournaments. I left the regional tournament with added confidence that I could keep winning, even in Madison. Thanks, Harry!

You're Not Normal!

Phil made many encouraging statements to John and me during our years together. One particular conversation permanently changed how I looked at accomplishing the goals I set for myself.

Earlier that year Phil had asked me what my goals were. I told him I wanted to study architecture, play college football, and win the state tournament.

"You are not normal!" was his reply.

No high school senior wants to be called abnormal and I was taken aback by his statement.

Seeing my bewilderment, he asked, "Has anyone else on your team set a goal to be a state champion?"

"Not that I know of," I replied.

"Do you know of anyone in any other sport who wants to be a state champion?" he questioned.

""I don't believe so," I answered. I knew some excellent athletes playing other sports in our high school, but I didn't know any who had the same goal I did to be a state champion.

Phil pressed further, "Do you know anyone in all of Cumberland who is training to be a state champion?"

I was getting his point. Based on the fact I had different goals than anyone else, I was not normal. Phil proceeded to tell me how I needed to sleep differently, wake up differently, eat differently, dress, go to school, train, wrestle, and study differently. The list was endless. All my decisions and choices would be made on a different basis because my goal was unique.

It became a common phrase around the house. "Ben, you can't eat that! You're not normal." "Ben, you have to go to bed early. You're not normal!" "You have to train more than anyone else because you're not normal." And on and on it went.

This new way of thinking helped me greatly when I faced

making choices about activities that were essentially good but might not help me realize my goals. Phil's illustration of being "not normal" has never left me and has kept me on target throughout my life in multiple situations.

Phil's confidence in me became very definite through our summer lifting times. After one particularly intense lift, he said, "Someday, Ben, you will go way past me in sports." That was important to me. Phil's sincerity was clear. For a long time I felt I had to get as fast, strong, big, and smart as Phil. I failed in all four. Five years later, after winning the Olympics, I knew his prediction had been fulfilled.

Life Beyond Wrestling

My academic studies in high school were up and down. After three years of taking average courses and getting average grades, my coaches, teachers, and advisors urged me to take college preparatory courses. Instead of more shop and drafting classes, I took calculus and physics, preparing me for my goal to be an architect someday. What really stretched me was college preparatory English. While enrolled in these new courses with the best students in my senior class, I gained new confidence as a student. But I also often felt I was just barely hanging on to this new and difficult ride that was going much faster than I had ever experienced.

Even our church pastor challenged me with something new. He asked me to teach a Sunday School class of fourth and fifth grade boys! Perhaps they controlled the class more often than I did. But in the end, this Sunday School teaching experience helped me put into my own words what I had learned from the Bible and what I believed about Jesus.

In all this, I learned some significant things. When you are young, stretch yourself and always try to do your best. This is the best way to prepare to stretch later in life. Do not be satisfied with just getting by. See how far your God-given talents can take you. You'll never know how far that is unless you dream big dreams, prepare yourself carefully and fully to reach those dreams, and give your best in all you do every day.

Keep your hopes and your dreams high, and keep them alive. And if your hopes and dreams are deferred:

- Look for what you can learn from past experiences,
- Make the necessary adjustments,
- Continue training hard and prepare fully,
- Get back in the game and compete with all you've got.

If you stay hopeful, you'll find new energy to meet the next challenge that comes your way. And you will progress to new levels.

—11—

DON'T WRESTLE LIKE A DEAD MAN ON A HORSE!

Young wrestlers do too much with their arms while ignoring their legs. This was true for me. My arms would get so tired they would ache with fatigue, yet I could seldom say the same for my legs. I needed to learn how to use the power my legs could provide.

I learned a number of moves that required my legs. My focus was too often on where to put them in a general sense while ignoring the precise placement required and the power they could provide. Using a "guillotine" or a "banana split" against a skilled opponent would get me into serious trouble because I was not using the force from my legs and my back to make the technique more powerful.

Coach Walsh taught us the leg turk. While riding an opponent from his left side, we would lift his near knee (his left leg) using our right hand, and then step under that near leg with our right leg and scoop up our opponent's right leg with our right leg. Then, if we arched our back, this would turn our opponent's hips and put us in a solid controlling position, allowing us to ride an opponent and look for back points. In time, I mastered the leg turk.

Unlike the leg turk, I struggled using the cross-body leg ride, even though it is much easier to apply than a leg turk. Whenever I would get my leg hooked for a cross-body ride, better opponents would easily counter it and put me on my back, or would at least put me in a bad wrestling position. I had not yet learned how to use the cross-body leg ride with the confidence needed to control a skilled opponent.

Sound Wrestling Instruction

Midway through my senior season, Mike Dutilly was home for the Christmas holidays from UW River Falls. I had known Mike since our grade school days when he was Tom's classmate. He was now a senior on his college wrestling team. Although Mike was not a starter, Coach Walsh introduced him with a definite tone of respect. He told us Mike was back in Cumberland on his Christmas break and that he wanted to train with us and help our team.

As practice continued, Mike walked around the room. He would stop here and there to watch my teammates, and then he would give them coaching pointers for improving. When he got to me, I noticed he was watching me for some time and looking at me wrestle from a number of different angles. But he made no comment about what he was seeing. When there was a break in the action, he calmly asked me a few questions:

"Ben, you're the team captain, aren't you?"

"You're a senior, right?"

"You're still undefeated this year, right?"

"You want to go to state again?"

"But this time you'd like to win the state championship, wouldn't you?"

"You want to wrestle somewhere in college, right?"

My answer to every one of these questions was, "Yes!"

Then Mike sternly told me that as he had been watching me work on the cross-body leg ride, my position and my technique were poor. In fact, he said, "Ben, your position and your technique stink." He told me if I wanted to keep winning and reach my wrestling goals, I needed to make some fundamental changes.

If I had not respected Mike and valued his opinion so much, I might have been offended by what he had just said to me. I may even have resisted his totally honest comments. Instead, I asked him to help me.

Over the next two or three practices, Mike repeatedly emphasized the need to be in positions of power and in positions of control whenever I used the cross-body leg ride. Most importantly, he showed me what those positions looked like compared to what I had been doing.

Until then, I really thought that just more hard work, just more running for better conditioning, and just more weight training for strength would make me a winning wrestler. But in those few days, Mike got me thinking about the importance of always having a sound wrestling position, good balance, control, and leg power. In other words, technique and sound positioning were important too, not just brute strength.

Mike taught me that instead of hooking my leg around an opponent's leg like a grapevine, I should instead hook just my heel inside my opponent's thigh. Additionally, instead of hugging or hooking my opponent with my arms, I should push his head and his shoulders away from me as I worked to turn his hips over for a pin. Instead of turning and looking toward my opponent, I should always arch my back and look away from him.

I learned I could protect myself while still forcing my opponent out of position. I had exposed myself to dangerous positions in an effort to force my opponent out of position.

Mike especially emphasized the need in leg riding for an arched back. He taught me to "sit up like a proud, confident cowboy, strong in the saddle" instead of "hanging limp over my opponent like a dead man on a horse."

This vivid image has stayed with me all these years. It's easy for anyone to visualize, easily remembered, and a great delight to teach to other wrestlers.

Applying My New Leg Wrestling Knowledge

After a few days, Mike went back to college and our team continued to practice. I do not remember anything in particular changing immediately in my wrestling because of Mike's coaching points until I got to the semifinals of the state tournament. Against a tall and powerful opponent, who also knew leg riding well, I got a reversal and then out-did him on leg riding enough to ride, control, and turn him for back points. I walked off the mat exhausted from the intense battle that I'd just fought, but I knew that the leg-riding technique I had learned earlier from Mike Dutilly had made all the difference in that match.

I will describe in later chapters how the aggressive use of leg riding earned me a scholarship to Iowa State University as well as many more opportunities.

Thank you!

I never again saw Mike Dutilly to thank him for what he had so carefully taught me. Some years later I met his son while he was in high school. I was saddened to learn from him that Mike was no longer living. When I told him what his dad had done for me, and when I expressed my heartfelt thanks, he beamed with pride. And he should be proud of his dad. Without Mike's wise and firmly communicated instruction, my wrestling career would likely have been much different.

—12—
STATE TOURNAMENT MEMORIES

Anyone who has ever competed in a state tournament has a story to tell. This was my second time at state and my previous trip had taught me a lot. My two losses, each by a pin, let me know state tournament competition is serious business.

Getting There

In February of 1968, the Wisconsin State Wrestling Tournament was a two-day event. There were sixteen qualified wrestlers entered in each weight class drawn from over 300 high schools across Wisconsin. In those days, we had just one division in the tournament. So whether you were from a big, mid-size, or small school, all wrestling teams competed for one team championship and all individual wrestlers competed for one individual championship in each weight class.

Leading up to the state meet, the field of wrestlers was narrowed, beginning with regional tournaments all around the state. From each regional, two wrestlers in each weight class qualified for a sectional tournament. There were eight sectional tournaments that would send two wrestlers in each weight class to the state meet in Madison. Since I won our sectional at 180 pounds, I was matched in the first round against a second place finisher from another sectional.

Coach Walsh and I, along with the other seniors on our team spent most of Thursday driving 250 miles from Cumberland to Madison. When we arrived, we went directly to the Field House where the tournament would be held on the UW Madison campus. I checked my weight, had a short workout, checked my weight again, and then ate just enough that evening to hold my weight until the next morning's weigh-in. That night, in the biggest hotel I'd ever been in, I slept quite well.

Day One - The Early Rounds

Early Friday morning, Coach Walsh and I went back to the Field House where I weighed in at just less than 182 pounds. To account for a wrestler's natural growth during the wrestling season, we were allowed two extra pounds in February.

We then went for breakfast and returned to the Field House. It was important to arrive early enough to allow plenty of time to warm up and get accustomed to the wrestling mats and the size of the Field House.

For the past twelve months, I'd pictured all this in my mind and I was eager to get back to the Field House. I knew I was much better prepared this time and I was anxious to prove to myself and others that a full year of hard training and competition had made me a much better wrestler.

Coach Walsh and I focused our full attention on winning each match, one by one: wrestling round one before thinking about round two, and then wrestling round two before thinking about round three.

Wanting to motivate me even more Coach told me, "Every win from now on, Ben, will be worth $1,000 to you." I laughed and brushed it off as his inference to a possible college scholarship. But later, I'd have to agree that his motivational prediction had some truth to it.

Although my first match was not easy, it was a good solid win. It was encouraging to be on the winning end! After a break, a meal, and a nap, I was back again for the evening round. Once more, a hard fought match gave me a solid win. Another year of wrestling experience, lifting weights, running for conditioning, and dreaming of wrestling success was paying off. I was not completely dominating the competitors at this level, but unlike the year before, I could control and wear down the best wrestlers in my weight class from around Wisconsin.

Day Two - Getting to the Finals

On Saturday morning, when I reported to weigh in for day

two, I was surprised to learn that I was two and a half pounds underweight. I must have been a bit anxious to lose that much overnight. Thinking that everyone else was big and strong, I was a little embarrassed as I prepared to weigh in. So I waited until after all the other wrestlers had gone through. I hoped maybe they would not see the scale tip for me at such a low weight.

But was I surprised! Watching each of the other seven wrestlers weigh in, it turned out I was the heaviest of all. It is amazing what sticks in our memories so many years later, and it is even more amazing what seems significant to us in our youth.

I wrestled a tall, strong opponent from Luxemburg-Casco in the semi-finals. Over the years, Luxemburg-Casco has been one of the most successful high school wrestling teams in the state. Early in the match, he put a cross-body leg ride on me. I had been unprepared for this move and for its punishing effect on my body the year before, but thanks to Mike Dutilly, I knew how to use it and how to defend against it.

To beat the Luxemburg-Casco wrestler, I knew I must get out from the bottom quickly. I also needed to get on top and ride him or he would ride me and get me so tired that I would no longer be a threat to him. After several attempts, I finished a switch and immediately began using the cross-body leg ride. I was already tired and not efficient at applying this move on an opponent of his caliber, so the match was hard fought throughout. Still, I was able to turn him for back points and won the match 7-0.

As the match ended, we were both exhausted. Afterward, I remember thinking every mile and every sprint I had run, plus all the weight lifting I had done in the past year, had all been well worth it.

Tired after winning in the semis, I caught my breath and began mentally preparing for my next match that evening, the state tournament finals! After briefly greeting my family, I ate lunch and took a nap. This was very important as I prepared for my finals match.

—13—

THE LONG-AWAITED FINALS AND LESSONS LEARNED FOR A LIFETIME

Going into the finals, my record was 28-0. I was about to cap off an undefeated season by winning the state championship, or I would end it with a loss. I entered the match determined to finish my season with a win.

My opponent, Rich Hinebaugh, was also undefeated at 26-0. He was a mature leader at Monroe High School, the son of a minister, a good student, and a disciplined person. His outstanding personal history earned him an appointment to the United States Air Force Academy in Colorado Springs. I had not forgotten Rich pinned me in the first round the year before, and I was determined not to let it happen again. He was the top-ranked wrestler in Wisconsin the entire season, and I needed to be ready. Almost every day for twelve months I had been consumed with beating him.

The Final Match

In the first period we each had some aggressive takedown attempts, but they were all "protected" attempts. Rich was far too experienced to overexpose himself to my takedown efforts. Toward the end of the first period, I maneuvered Rich into a vulnerable position and threw him to his back. With all his experience and knowledge, he ended up out-of-bounds and no points were awarded.

As the second period began, I was on the bottom. The whizzer was a wrestling move I commonly used. I had full confidence in it, both defensively on my feet and offensively for earning an escape from the bottom. Rich rode me with his right arm strongly around my waist. His riding position felt like I could use a whizzer on him, and so I did. Pulling myself slightly away from him and hooking my left arm over his right arm, I got the whizzer. Continuing to work it, I pulled my hips out from under him and began to tripod on both of my feet and my free hand. Soon my hips were free. I felt ready to break away for a one-point escape.

Since I felt so much freedom with my hips, I thought to myself, "Why not go for a two-point reversal instead of just a one-point escape?" I moved back in toward Rich and stepped over him with my left leg. In response, he immediately raised his hips and drove over me, forcing me under him and to my back. His arm was still strongly around me. It was a simple maneuver for him to squeeze me with all the weight of his chest. Instantly, he pinned me.

Just that quickly, it was all over. My frantic attempts to undo my elementary error barely had time to start. My beginner's mistake ended my climb up the mountain within inches of the peak. In a matter of seconds, twelve long months of dreaming about a state championship and working hard toward that goal were now over.

My Reaction

I faced my coach, picked up my warm-up jacket, which now seemed as heavy as the two heavyweights still wrestling, and worked my way back to the locker room. I hoped maybe this was just a nightmare and soon I would wake up. For now though, I just wanted to avoid everyone and shed some tears somewhere alone.

My twelve months of dreaming, the hard training that went with those dreams, coming so close to reaching my goal only to have it end so quickly because of my foolish elementary mistake, and my family's sincere interest in seeing me compete all worked together to make this finals match the most memorable one in all my sixteen years of competition. Although I worked harder, longer, and smarter four years later as I prepared for the Munich Olympics, I do not think I have ever worked with more eagerness than I did for that high school state championship. My efforts got me all the way to the finals, but they did not get me the top prize.

Had I failed? Yes, of course, I had failed. I failed to reach my immediate goal. But I also knew that over the past year I had greatly improved as a wrestler. All the many hours of work were still worthwhile even though I now hurt so badly.

My disappointing loss in the finals of the state tournament taught me some very important lessons and confirmed key relationships with others who have helped me over a lifetime.

1. Dreaming ahead, committing ourselves fully to the task at hand, and working hard to complete that task changes us for the better. This will result in lasting benefit from the efforts we make, even if our goal is not reached.
2. The more we dream about, plan for, and work hard toward something significant, the more we will hurt if we fail to achieve it. But even when we fail, the discipline we develop matures us, making our dreams, plans, and efforts still worthwhile.
3. If we trust Him to do so, God can bring good out of our disappointments and failure.
4. At key turning points in life, the love and commitment of those most dear to us can be confirmed.
5. There are no guaranteed wins in sports - you can't buy a state wrestling title with money or hard work! You can only put yourself in a position to make the probabilities greater.

I see that much good has come to me, and others around me, because I did my best to win a state championship, even though I lost in the finals.

My family would give me repeated words of encouragement. I believe they did so in part because they saw how committed I was to finding a way to win. I knew the hard work was having a positive effect when others could confidently share compliments on what they saw.

—14—
FAMILY SUPPORT AND BROTHERLY RESPECT

I am often asked "What motivated you to remain so dedicated in your wrestling and to stay competing for sixteen years?" This chapter may offer a partial answer to that question.

Phil's Encouragement

I have many fond memories of every member of our family helping me in some way with my wrestling. As a grade school boy, I was especially impressed with Phil. He was my "big brother" who wrestled and also played football, baseball, ran track, and excelled in his studies. I often found myself wanting to follow in his footsteps by doing well in both school and sports.

During my elementary school years, I recall Phil being way too pushy and too demanding of his younger brothers. No doubt, we referred to him as a bully more than once. He often demanded we play baseball with him, which was fine for a while, but the intensity and the length of those baseball sessions often went beyond what either John or I could reasonably take as grade school boys.

Only after I was in high school and Phil was away at college did I fully appreciate his example. By then, he was a varsity football player at the University of Wisconsin and continued to do well in his academic studies with plans to be a lawyer. Then it was great to be known as "Phil's little brother."

It took me awhile to match the intensity of Phil's workouts: after all, he was training for Big Ten football. The summer before my senior year was invaluable as he made time around his law school preparation to help me train in hopes of a football scholarship and a state wrestling championship.

In late September of my senior year, Phil left for basic training in the Army at Fort Campbell, Kentucky. After nearly every one of my wrestling matches that season, Phil would write or call and usually talk to Mom about how I was doing in wrestling and in school. Later I realized that these updates helped him as he was going through the drudgery of everyday Army life. At the time, I did not realize how encouraging hearing about my wrestling was for him.

State Tournament

The morning after I qualified for the state tournament, Phil called and talked to Mom. He confirmed that he planned to fly from Fort Knox to Madison to attend the state tournament, and he would see us on Friday. His Army pass and airline tickets for the trip were all in order. I was really excited that he would be there!

As I warmed up for my first match on Friday, John brought me some disappointing news. He said Phil was not going to make it to the tournament as he had planned. His Army training schedule had changed at the last minute, and a mandatory physical fitness test would not be completed until Saturday noon. All off-base passes for his company were postponed until then.

I was disappointed, of course, but I knew the obvious thing to do was concentrate on wrestling and to win as many matches as I could. This would be the most encouraging thing for Phil.

Phil realized that if he stayed for the Saturday morning test, he would not get to Madison to see me wrestle at all. So he decided he would leave Kentucky early Friday evening, arriving in Madison around 10:00 pm that night.

Early Saturday morning, to my surprise, John and I saw Phil in the lobby of our hotel. He looked a little rough and very tired from traveling late the night before, but it was great to see him. After a brief conversation, Phil left with John to take a shower and get some rest. I left to weigh in, not knowing all Phil had gone through to get from Kentucky to Madison for the tournament.

Dad, Mom, Becky, and three of my four brothers were all in the Field House that night to watch me wrestle for the championship. Everybody was there except Tom who was in the Army stationed in South Korea. They saw me wrestle and saw me lose. I knew they would be disappointed for me, but I also knew that deep down inside they were proud of my second place finish. They had all supported the effort I put into making it that far. I was concerned about how Phil would handle my loss.

After the match was over, I needed somewhere alone to deal with my huge setback. Heading through the bleachers toward the locker room, I saw Phil coming down the bleacher stairs. What could I say to him? I did not know. All I could think was that I had disappointed my big brother. As he walked slowly down the stairs, he saw me. When he reached the floor, he turned away.

It was at that moment I saw my 23-year-old big brother was crying! After a moment he walked over to me. We hurt together and cried together. And then he assured me that he was enormously proud of me as his little brother.

The memory of that moment has come back to me many times. Win, lose, or draw, I would never quit. When I have been in a tough match, feeling too tired to continue, the thought of Phil crying there with me in our disappointment would come to mind. Then I would go back to work with increased energy. No matter how much it hurt to go on, I would not quit. I never again wanted to see my big brother, my friend, my coach, my hero disappointed because of my failure.

The next morning, our family took Phil to the airport for his return flight to Kentucky. As he waited to board the plane, comments were made about him facing his company commander after he got back to Fort Knox. Phil said goodbye, waved to us, and then climbed the stairs to the airplane. As he did, I turned to John and asked, "What's this all about?"

John seemed surprised at my question. "You don't know about how Phil came to the state tournament?" he asked.

"No," I said. "What's going on?"

John explained how Phil had come to Madison after all off-base travel for his company was postponed until Saturday afternoon. Phil had disobeyed orders when he left early Friday without a pass to cover his travels, and he had been nervous about the military police confronting him while he was away. He was ready to face his commanding officer and pay the price for his travels when he returned on Sunday. For several weeks, Phil was confined to his Army barracks and to the immediate training area nearby and was required to do a lot of cleaning up in the company area.

Phil had concluded that flying to Madison to see me wrestle in the state tournament was worth the penalty that he would have to pay when he got back to Fort Knox. He has always been quick to say that he would not have come if security would have been compromised. During the tournament, Phil sat quietly, mostly up in the high bleachers. I did not quite know why at the time, but there are lots of things that even a high school senior does not understand about his big brother.

Brotherly Respect

One thing I was sure of, Phil and I had spent a lot of time working together and dreaming the same big dreams training and competing hard to try and reach them. We had developed a strong mutual respect. It was a deep respect that has continued undiminished over the years. And no wrestling loss, no matter how disappointing to us at the time, could lessen that respect.

—15—

FROM DISAPPOINTMENT TO SUCCESS

The compliments I received after my second-place finish in the state tournament eased some of the pain left by my mistake. The disappointment I felt both for myself and my family had me wondering if all my hard work was really worth it.

My goal to earn a college football scholarship faded with each loss. Now in the same way, my dream to wrestle in college seemed limited after my loss in the finals at state. I thought to myself, "What college or university wrestling coach would want a second place finisher?" Today I understand that individual losses do not necessarily need to end opportunities.

The twenty-plus letters that Coach Walsh had sent to college and university wrestling coaches now seemed like a waste of his time. He had written to colleges and universities that offered both wrestling and a degree in architecture.

Olympic Freestyle Preparation

There were many negative thoughts on my part, but my optimistic coach was not done yet. He had another idea. The regional Olympic trials for freestyle wrestling were scheduled to be held in a couple of weeks in River Falls, Wisconsin. This was less than an hour away from Comstock! Coach Walsh asked me, "Why don't you go, Ben? Maybe a college coach will see you."

Why not?? Because I had never even seen a freestyle match before, let alone wrestled in one. That's why not!

Olympic wrestling has two distinct styles: freestyle and Greco-Roman, and the rules are different than American high school wrestling (commonly known as folkstyle.) In the summer of 1967, Coach Walsh had taken John and me to watch the Pan-Am Greco-

Roman trials in Coon Rapids, Minnesota. Greco-Roman is very different from our high school and college styles, and freestyle is quite different as well. For me to compete in the Olympic trials, I would need to adjust to an unfamiliar style of wrestling.

Although I was hesitant at first, my persistent coach had already given some thought to my need to adjust. A clinic in River Falls to teach area wrestlers the freestyle rules and moves was set for a week before the trials. I could learn the freestyle rules and the moves, and still have a full week to drill and practice before the tournament. John recalls us meeting National Greco-Roman Coach Alan Rice at the River Falls clinic.

For my week of drilling and practice, Coach Walsh and I had to arrange for both a practice area and a practice routine. Our wrestling room (which was also the stage) was now all set up for the spring play, so a mat for wrestling practice was unavailable for me there. But Coach Walsh, who was also the head track coach, decided that the two 4'x10' pads hanging on the gym walls just behind the school's basketball rims could be laid out on the gym floor to serve as my makeshift wrestling mat.

I practiced in the high school gym on this make-do mat, while the pole vaulters, shot putters, and baseball team worked out all around me. I was conspicuous for sure, but I was determined to give this wrestling opportunity my best effort.

My tiny 8x10 foot "mat," with a joint in the middle, worked fine for drilling my new freestyle moves. Gary Mathias, a wrestling teammate, joined me a couple times when he was free from working on his family's farm. Brian Kamnetz, a shot putter on our track team, had never wrestled, but he drilled moves with me in exchange for me agreeing to practice throwing the shot. Some of my other partners had never wrestled before either.

Practicing the new Olympic freestyle moves, perfecting new skills, and developing my timing were all important. And I also did some running and weight training to stay in good physical shape.

One night that week, I joined John an hour away in Menomonie for practice with some of his UW Stout teammates. While there, my clumsiness caused me to injure an eyelid of the Stout heavyweight. John and I visited him later in the doctor's office while he got some stitches. What a bizarre week!

Regional Competition Day

I entered the tournament with a real curiosity about this new style of wrestling. Everyone in my weight class (191 pounds) had only high school experience, and I beat each wrestler I faced using mainly a basic double-leg takedown and the cross-body leg ride. The leg ride enabled me to turn my opponents for back points or even a pin. In the finals, I met a wrestler who, although stronger than the others, had been out of school for a year. Again, all my hard conditioning paid off.

I would later train with this wrestler's younger brother, Pete Liskow, while he was attending UW Madison.

John also wrestled in this same Olympic trials tournament. Unlike my weight class, he met up with some experienced freestylers and finished third. This tournament showed both of us what top-notch freestyle wrestling is all about. That day we saw some of the most intense wrestling matches we had ever seen. John went back to Stout somewhat humbled by his experience, but also a bit wiser about the opportunities available in Olympic wrestling.

National Olympic Trials in Ames

After the Wisconsin regional trials were over I returned home thinking that wrestling in the Olympic trials was just an interesting experience that would not lead anywhere. Conversely, Coach Walsh went home thinking about a way to raise the needed money for me to wrestle in the national trials in Ames, Iowa!

Sensing fear about the level of wrestling I would face at the tournament, I blurted out, "Coach, I can't win that tournament!"

"I know that, Ben. But maybe a college coach will see you." His honest and realistic reply has always impressed me.

Two weeks later, in Dad's car and with a borrowed singlet, Coach Walsh and I were off on the eight-hour drive to Ames. The tournament was hosted by Iowa State University and its head wrestling coach, Harold Nichols and assistant, Les Anderson. This tournament selected the members of the 1968 Freestyle Team that would represent the United States at the Mexico City Olympics.

Arriving in Ames the afternoon before the tournament, I loosened up on the mats and checked my weight. Meanwhile, Coach

Walsh went looking for the Iowa State coaches. Finding Les Anderson in his office, Coach Walsh promptly brought me to meet him.

Outside Coach Anderson's office, I saw the many wall plaques identifying and describing Iowa State's athletic All Americans. I noticed the biggest share of them were wrestlers. Coach Anderson and Dan Gable were among them. I could clearly see the long-standing excellence of Iowa State's wrestling program.

Competition began the next day. My first-round opponent was Russ Camilleri of California. Russ was a 29 year-old veteran who had been a member of three U.S. World Freestyle Teams and two Greco-Roman Olympic Teams. After he scored a couple times, I scored a takedown. Then Russ took me down and turned me for back points, and he did it all with such ease. He finished me off with a pin, but I have never forgotten his encouraging words afterward. "Ben, you keep wrestling. You could do very well." Positive words from a seasoned veteran can mean a lot to a young hungry competitor.

I have often thanked him for those words when our paths have crossed, usually at the NCAA Division 1 Championships held each year in March.

My second-round opponent was Chuck Jean, a freshman wrestler at Iowa State. Coach Walsh was excited about me wrestling Chuck because he thought that both coaches, Nichols and Anderson, would be there watching and this could be a big opportunity for me to impress them. Coach Walsh told me that both coaches believed Chuck had exceptional wrestling talent and that he had the potential to be an excellent wrestler for Iowa State. This ended up being very true down the road.

For most of the first period, Chuck and I sparred on our feet. When I thought he seemed distracted and not totally focused on the match, I attacked him with a hard double-leg takedown. I immediately put in a cross-body leg ride and used the guillotine to roll Chuck across his back scoring two points for me but also giving up two points to Chuck. The period ended with Chuck on his back.

In the second and third periods, he really went to work on me. For the remainder of the match, I was fighting for my life and I lost 9-3. As I walked off the mat I felt I had missed another great opportunity. One minute my opponent is on his back, and the next minute I am fighting to avoid being pinned. How can that be impressive?

After the match, Coach Walsh had me meet Coach Nichols. We spoke briefly, and then I headed dejectedly to the locker room. Coach Walsh tried to be hopeful as we traveled home, but it was really hard to imagine how I could ever get a college wrestling scholarship after my two one-sided losses in Ames.

After returning home, I told Mom that I sure would like to attend Iowa State University even if they did not offer me a scholarship. But we both wondered how I would ever be able to pay the bills. I loved the campus. It helps that spring comes in Ames much earlier than it does in northern Wisconsin, and that Iowa State also offers a degree in architecture.

In response to Coach Walsh's many letters to college coaches all around the country, I received some positive letters. I even made an all-expense-paid recruiting trip to the University of Washington in Seattle. But no one offered me a scholarship, so I began thinking more about enrolling in a smaller college and about maybe not studying architecture after all.

The Call of a Lifetime

About two weeks after my trip to Iowa State, the telephone rang at 7 a.m. as I was getting ready for school. Mom answered it and called up the stairs to say the phone was for me. Was I surprised! It was Coach Nichols calling to say he would send me the papers for a partial scholarship if I would like to attend Iowa State and wrestle for the Cyclones. I told him I was definitely interested!

After much discussion with Mom, Dad, John, our pastor, Coach Walsh, and a few others, and after looking to God's Word for wisdom and direction on this important decision, I signed and returned the scholarship papers to Coach Nichols. With that, I was now on my way to becoming a part of the Big Eight Conference powerhouse, the Iowa State University Cyclones! I would now get the chance to wrestle and study architecture in college. I had reached, at the time, my athletic and academic goals!

Why did Coach Nichols offer me a college wrestling scholarship anyway? I can't say for sure, but I asked him years later why he did not recruit someone who had actually won a state championship or maybe even won two or three state championships. After all, Iowa State's reputation allowed it to recruit the very best, and I was clearly not the best. He replied that it seemed I really, truly wanted to attend Iowa State and that I really wanted to study architecture. To him, desire in a college wrestler was essential. Beyond that, he liked my aggressiveness in taking down Chuck Jean with a strong double-leg and transitioning to a pin.

I have often said this story of mine has *God's fingerprints* all over it. Despite all the mistakes and disappointments, God added His blessing to my efforts. He caused something good, really much better than I could have reasonably hoped for or could have imagined, to come out of my failed efforts. My experience in the 1968 Olympic trials opened a door of opportunity that almost seemed unreal.

Coach Walsh and me with the poster boy that announced our wrestling matches in the high school entry. This is the picture that made the front cover of *Amateur Wrestling News* magazine. Note Coach's foot cast.

Wrestling awards our junior-senior year.

High school football uniforms with John and Dad.

1968 Wisconsin State place winners.

Above: 1968 State Chamionships
Rich Hinebaugh, Monroe - 1st,
Me - 2nd,
Tom Watry, Port Washington - 3rd
& Joe Wade, Portage - 4th.

Right: Homemade weight
bench - Phil's creation.

John's senior year.

College Wrestling

—16—

GOOD NEWS FROM AFAR MY FRESHMAN YEAR - ISU 1968-‘69

It's hard to imagine how anyone could have been more naïve than I was coming out of a small rural community and going off to college at a large state university. It was easy to see we were on the edge of many things and a long way from the mainstream of American life.

When I first arrived at Iowa State, it seemed to me that, at best, I was only on the fringe of the wrestling team. Nearly everyone with a scholarship was a state champion, and over half of them were state champions more than once. What was I doing in the Iowa State practice room? I was only a second-place finisher.

However, I knew right away that I wanted to be a part of that wrestling team, and I determined to work as hard and as smart as I could along with the rest of those young men.

One thing I soon noticed about the upperclassmen was they had an unsettled, discontented attitude. Although they had finished second in the nation as a team the season before and had three individual national champions, Dale Bahr, Reggie Wicks, and Dan Gable, my teammates talked as though we were still miles from the top. It was very clear they wanted badly to get there!

Throughout the 1960s, Iowa State had finished near the top in major college wrestling. From 1960 through 1968, Iowa State had finished first once, second four times, and third three times.

At first, I did not fully comprehend the significance of my team's past successes. I did not understand the standard of wrestling excellence that the NCAA Championships set each year for our team. And it surely never occurred to me that soon I would be helping maintain that standard of excellence.

Iowa State's two wrestling coaches, Nichols and Anderson, deserve the credit in those years for creating and maintaining Iowa State's standard of excellence. In a letter I sent to Phil in early December, I wrote, "I really like Coach Nichols and our assistant, Coach Anderson. They really know their stuff, and treat you like you were their own son."

Months of Hard Training

My teammates built a strong foundation for the national tournament by putting in months of hard training throughout the year. When Coach Nichols was asked about the prospects for the Cyclone team, this man of few words summed up his thoughts and hopes for the new season by simply saying, "They've got great work habits, and they work well together."

As my freshman season began, I was also working hard to get off to a good start as a student. That was my highest priority, even higher than working for success as a wrestler. The only way I could imagine myself actually competing as a member of the Iowa State team was to still be around after all the others had graduated. I was not even close to beating any varsity wrestler, so I only wrestled that year in one freshman dual meet and in two or three open tournaments.

Nothing I saw that season as a young freshman gave me any reason to believe that this Iowa State team, which I saw in practice every day, would beat the perennial wrestling powers, Oklahoma State University and the University of Oklahoma. Early that season, we placed second behind Michigan State at the annual Midlands Tournament, but that was without either Oklahoma school participating. I knew my team was near the top in college wrestling, but I also knew we were not yet there.

During that freshman year, I learned of the intense Iowa State rivalry with Oklahoma and Oklahoma State. In our home-and-away dual meets with these two schools, we split with each of them. I was told this occasionally happened but that, more often than not, we would lose both of our dual meets to both of the Oklahoma schools. This, at least, was an improvement.

Iowa State hosted the Big Eight Conference Tournament that

year. I eagerly watched it all, trying to take in all I could about the tournament. We finished third, and it seemed we were near the top in college wrestling but still behind both Oklahoma schools.

The National Wrestling Championships

Finally, our season was near its end. Our team left for the 1969 NCAA National Championships at Brigham Young University in Provo, Utah. I recall our team members quietly packing for the trip and then heading off to the Des Moines airport while the rest of us wished them well and went back to class. As I think on it, there was nothing at all unusual about our team's send-off: no trumpet blasts and no fanfare. Our team simply packed its bags and went off to Utah to do what it was supposed to do while everyone else on campus remained busy with their everyday class responsibilities.

The next day, we began to hear reports and it was news that they were doing well. We heard Dan Gable was pinning everyone. At first, it was almost an interruption to hear this. We had our own schoolwork to do.

Next thing we know, the tournament was over and Iowa State had won the national championship!

Not only had we won it, we scored more points than any other team in the history of the NCAA meet. We scored 104 points, far ahead of second place Oklahoma's 69.

ISU had three national champions - Dan Gable, Jason Smith, and Chuck Jean - and we had eight All Americans. (An All-American was someone who placed in the top six.) To top it off, Gable was voted the Outstanding Wrestler and won the trophy for having the most pins.

Welcome Home, National Champions!

The one event in all this that affected me most directly was the welcome home for our team. Late Sunday evening, the team flew back from Utah to Iowa, arriving on campus well after dark. News spread throughout the college dormitories that there would be a welcome home rally in the old State Gym.

Another freshman teammate and I arrived early. We got good seats while they were still setting up the chairs. The chairs filled up quickly and students began standing anywhere they could find space, in the back, on the sides, and even up on the overhanging running track.

There was a lot of excitement in the State Gym that night! First, the cheerleaders came in and led us all in a couple of cheers. Then in came our team: my teammates, our coaches, and the student manager walking in through the doorway, one by one.

I can clearly recall my thoughts. "I know these guys! That's my team! They're ordinary men facing all the problems of the late '60s, just like everyone else." But then I thought, "These are normal people, but they've taken their abilities and have faithfully worked hard and worked smart for a long time, and as a result, they've outdone everyone else. And now they're the national champions. *And if they can be the best, then it's possible for me to be the best!"*

My Determination to Wrestle at My Best

That night my hope and my confidence about my future in wrestling rose 200%. I began believing that I could become one of the top wrestlers in the nation. It seemed entirely reasonable for me to dream and work hard toward winning a national championship, both as a member of the team and as an individual. I determined that night to work hard and work smart to gain a spot on our varsity wrestling team for the next season. Almost without realizing it, my expectations shifted from waiting until the better wrestlers graduated to becoming determined to help Iowa State win the nationals again next year.

The experience of watching my team compete from far away reminds me of the words from Scripture, *"As cold water to a weary soul, so is good news from a far country." Proverbs 25:25*

I was greatly encouraged by the news I heard from a distance about our team. When I heard about their success, saw my teammates walking in one by one, and saw them standing there before us in the old State Gym with their big sheepish grins, I knew that all their hard work had paid off. They had upset the perennial powers in college wrestling from Oklahoma and Oklahoma State. I knew right then that it would be worthwhile for me to work as hard as I could to do the same.

—17—
INCREDIBLE WRESTLING PARTNERS

My first two years at Iowa State exposed me to one of the best college wrestling rooms in America. This room is an essential part of how I became a 2-time national champion and an Olympian. I have always marveled at the talent, skill, determination, and hard work I saw on the ISU team. Coach Nichols and Les Anderson had clearly been doing their homework for years to assemble men with natural ability and a desire to win.

These men were far from perfect, but they desired to excel and were hungry for a national championship. Their credentials are impressive, and the attitudes and perspectives they bestowed on me were equally impressive.

Head Coach Harold Nichols was a 1939 NCAA champion for the University of Michigan. In his coaching, he chose an austere approach in many ways. He was a man of few words, but was always thinking and planning. He did an incredible job of setting the stage for our team and led us like a general who could see the big picture. Though many called him "Nick" I could not quite bring myself to comfortably call him that. Coach never demanded our respect. We just wanted to respect him.

It would be my senior year before I conversed very much with Coach Nichols. After my graduation, grad school, and years of being a coach, we conversed more freely. My shyness limited our early conversations, but not my respect for him. His wife, Ruth, was always such a sweet and kind lady. She got me talking a little earlier.

Coach wrestled with us, but only down on the mat. He was in his fifties and created a patient, controlled pace at which to work while we learned riding, pinning, escapes, and reversals. Although

I was bigger than him, he totally controlled me at first. Slowly, I started reversing him and then riding him. Coach's pace was slow and methodical in order for us to feel each position, and we wrestled with our minds as much as our bodies. Not a lot needed to be said unless he wanted to explain a move. I observed he was watching every position I chose. Long before I became a winning asset to the team, Coach Nichols patiently waited and watched me. His patience helped me build confidence.

Assistant Coach Les Anderson was a 2-time NCAA champion for Iowa State and Coach Nichols. He was the personable coaching partner Nichols needed. Les was a good communicator, respected, and a quality organizer. His techniques were just what I needed for going to another level in my wrestling. Les was smaller, so he wrestled full-go with anyone under 150 pounds. I do not recall drilling or wrestling with Les much at all, but I had many conversations about techniques and positioning with him. He was the kind of coach who loved taking those extra minutes to talk through techniques and help us through sticking points.

Meeting his children came in time and I had several brief conversations with his wife. She worked as a checkout clerk at the HyVee grocery store just across the street from my dorm.

Years later, Coach Anderson said: **"I never tore anyone down in order to build them back up."** That made all the sense in the world and a major difference for us as developing wrestlers. Many coaches badger and belittle their wrestlers, and that approach is easy and natural to fall into. Les and Nichols had gotten past that style. There were no loud commands or belittling people in the practice room. They treated us as gentlemen and conversed directly with respect. I believe they succeeded in creating an atmosphere that was comfortable and pleasant. We all came and worked harder than I had ever imagined young men could, and it was super enjoyable to be part of that team.

Coach Bobby Douglas was a 2-time Olympian and a World Bronze Medalist. He came as a graduate student and assistant coach. The Iowa State upperclassmen had a hard time giving him their full respect because Coach Douglas had wrestled his senior season at Oklahoma State. I heard more than one comment about him being an "Okie" who could not be trusted. Douglas was patient and just kept coaching people and wrestling hard with us. With time we began to see he really knew his technique and was glad to share his knowledge.

I believe Coach Douglas was a key factor in the way I learned to counter leg attacks and do freestyle turns. He was tall and lanky like me and our legs could get us in trouble. He taught me to sprawl my legs away, turn the angle and attack for my own takedown and then back points.

Part of Coach Douglas' graduate work was to create a book called *Wrestling - The Making of a Champion: The Takedown.* He asked several of us to help demonstrate moves for the photographs that fill the book. Well before I was winning for ISU, he had me in a book that became the standard takedown manual for many wrestlers. I enjoyed the way he organized and described each maneuver.

Tom Peckham was a 2-time NCAA champion for Iowa State and placed fourth at 191 pounds in the 1968 Mexico City Olympics the summer before I arrived. Tom was a volunteer coach for our team and also employed by Coach Nichols who ran a wrestling equipment company. They sold just about any equipment wrestlers needed. Peckham sold mats, headgear, shoes, and knee pads. He also coordinated several ladies to make warmups and the three-piece uniforms high school and college wrestlers wore. I remember stopping by the store once and being shown a completely new headgear they were working to develop.

Tom was much stronger than me, but not much heavier. We wrestled often in practice. I never scored a point on Tom. He was simply a tough, stubborn, determined wrestler. I do not remember him bullying his way on the mat. He did not need to. He was thoughtful of his position and kicked his stubborn determination up a notch when absolutely necessary.

One day late in the season of my freshman year I got in really deep on a double leg and finally thought I had Tom in a takedown. Instead, he called on that determination, settled his hips and drove them down and through me. My ankle was caught with no place to go and was sprained badly. I had a week out of practice getting the swelling down, and several weeks of taping it. I took time to recall that I had left myself vulnerable when I thought I had won the position. I knew I had a long way to go in the sport to defeat men like Tom. Wrestling with him helped me greatly.

Tom was personable and positive, and a good conversationalist. Laughing and apologizing for injuring me, he encouraged me to keep working. My desire to train in the spring for freestyle while daily taping the sprained ankle, showed him I wanted to learn. I recall getting more than one compliment from him that spring. His knowledge of freestyle was also invaluable for my hunger to improve. Part way through my sophomore season he moved away and it would be two years before we crossed paths again.

Jim Duschen wrestled at 191 pounds and heavyweight. Jim was a Big Eight champion and an All-American. He won most matches at heavyweight, but for big events he cut hard to make 191 pounds. He was bigger than me and a true "Charles Atlas" muscle man. Many have commented that Jim looked like he was chiseled from granite. For all his physical presence, Jim was friendly, quiet, and contemplative.

He could easily beat me, but he was a senior and probably anxious to stop cutting weight. So my learning curve was rising much faster than his. Taking him down was almost impossible at first. Scoring a point here and there from the bottom was easier and brought my first compliments from him.

We wrestled often in practice. Time after time Jim out-muscled me. But something began to change. One by one, I learned to avoid those muscle positions. Slowly, I began to learn how to deflect his power and weight. One day Jim had me down under him after blocking my double leg takedown attempt. He was in front, holding me with his arms around my chest to keep me under him. But that day I felt him unable to control me sideways. Clamping his arms to my chest I rolled him sideways and put him on his back (a barrel roll in wrestling language.) I held him there while he kicked like a turtle on its back. That day was significant for me. I had learned how to take away the strength of a super strong man and put him in trouble. That memory has been clear in my mind ever since. I had put him in a position where he could not use his strength.

Jim was quiet, even shy, so I thought him aloof as a senior from a new freshman like me. Later we would talk freely. But that whole first year it was your typical respectful freshman-senior relationship. Increasingly, Jim was an encouragement by his compliments. I was slowly beginning to think of moving up from 177 pounds where I was cutting weight and could not beat Chuck Jean. When Jim graduated, I would take my chances moving up to try the 190 pound weight class.

Carl Adams wrestled at 150 pounds, and later 158 pounds. He became a 2-time NCAA champion and U.S. World Team member. Being in my class, I watched him develop step by step just like I had to. Carl got a jump start on me our freshman year by making varsity right from the beginning and winning most of his matches. It seemed to me the only time he faltered in continual improvement was our sophomore year when he failed to place at nationals. But he took that loss in stride and charged through our junior season to a national championship.

Carl worked hard and was consistent and faithful in his training. His stability was a reminder to me to keep training and learning, and good things will happen. Even though I seldom wrestled Carl, his strong, calm, growing confidence and domination on his feet was an important positive example to me. I will speak more of Carl in future chapters.

Dave Martin was an NCAA runner-up as a junior and a champion his senior year at 158 pounds. Dave is a talker. He was positive and fun almost all of the time, so his consistent talk was encouraging and entertaining. I just listened at the beginning because he was a fast enough thinker to turn any comment into a jab at you. I think Dave's light-hearted fun talk was good even when we were the brunt of his jokes. He relaxed a lot of stressful settings. When we get together even today, Dave can entertain us and out-talk us all.

Dave wrestled a lot with Gable, Carl Adams, and Jason Smith. His friendship with Gable was very strong from the beginning. Dave was good at rolling his opponents and a great rider. If he did not get a takedown he would work his opponents on the mat. I took note of that because my takedowns did not always work either. So I, too, learned to win down on the mat.

Dave and I wrestled some. He easily beat me at first, but by my sophomore year Dave was complaining about my clumsiness. I took it as a compliment since he was finding it harder to control me.

Jason Smith was a 2-time national champion at 167 pounds. He was super talented with natural strength, quickness, and smoothness. He was a thinker and he analyzed everything on and off the mat.

I soon realized that whenever I wrestled with Jason I should not get emotional or crazy. The longer we stayed methodical the better. Once he got going and focused his mind fully on the workout, I was toast. His movements could be so smooth and effortless, and when he really meant business his speed left me in the dust and his strength put me in deep trouble. I remember specifically learning to start practice slowly with Jason, look for a chance to score, and ride him as long and as hard as I could. When he got out, he would be all business. Jason could turn his focus on and off instantly. I learned the value of smoothness and focus with Jason.

Chuck Jean was a 2-time national champion at 177 pounds. Chuck was very short and broad. He could easily gain weight and needed to lose a lot the morning of meets. I believe he improved his shape early in the season by the long hard workouts to make weight.

Chuck was very strong. Bear hugs were a major strength of his. He would influence me greatly with that move. Stepping from an underhook to an arm around the back, to locked hands around the chest while positioning hips for control, was done step by step. Chuck made it look so easy and crushed my ribs many times with that move. Because he was short, he could get right under people and close to his opponent. For a long time I did not see how bear hugs could work for me. But by the time I was a senior, I was doing the same move. With time, my long arms permitted me to get around my opponents, and the bear hug became a key move for me throughout all nine years of international wrestling.

At first I thought Chuck was quiet. During practice he would be all business. And when he was cutting weight he would get quiet. But before very long I found him very talkative. And as his success and confidence grew with the older wrestlers, he showed himself able to converse with the best. Chuck was considerate of others. He was a sophomore and an underclassman like me, and defended me more than once against the ribbings of the upperclassmen. I appreciated and needed that.

Dan Gable was a 2-time NCAA champion at 142 pounds. What a privilege it was to watch Dan in person at the peak of his competitive career. He was captain of the team and a returning NCAA champion when I arrived. He was much lighter than me but I kept seeing him wrestle with the same people I was. Jason, Chuck, and even Tom Peckham were on his daily workout partner list. Why was he going with much bigger men so often? My conclusion is that Dan did not want to win just his weight class, he wanted to keep learning and improving in all aspects of the game as much as possible. Therefore, he wanted to wrestle with the toughest wrestlers as often as possible.

Many people talk of Gable's wrestling style as "always forward," "never retreating," and "in your face." That was not fully true of the way Dan wrestled. He went in every direction. It depended on which direction would expose his opponent's weakness. This was obvious to me when he began asking to wrestle with me. No angle or direction was closed to him. When working with much bigger wrestlers he had to adjust to avoid our strength and weight. I describe his style, I think more accurately, as "relentless."

Regarding the "in your face" approach, Dan wrestled with enthusiasm and confidence, but it was not like a grudge or spiteful fight. In fact, I remember Dan approaching practice and each match more like a chess game where it is important to be fully alert, thoughtful, and always attacking to keep your opponent from getting his strategy started.

In summary, I tell people I am the most blessed man to ever step on a wrestling mat. How could I, or anyone else, have known that these ten men would be in the practice room and that they knew, or were learning, a mindset that would make them the best team in America two times? During that time, the Iowa State wrestling room was producing three national champions each year.

I began to notice something from these men: they were advanced and very confident. They could give compliments and encourage younger wrestlers, knowing they were so far ahead of us that we would not catch up with them before they graduated and were gone.

Looking back, I believe the biggest thing was their confidence. They were not selfish about their skills or overly haughty. They were all confident enough to compliment others knowing they knew techniques that could win and that they had prepared physically to be able to compete with anyone. That confidence became contagious to us younger men.

I encourage young wrestlers to **find a place where you get pushed to failure repeatedly. Learn to survive and build confidence until you can become the leader yourself. Find the opportunity and stay at it long enough to master it.**

—18—

A YOUNG WRESTLER'S INCONSISTENCY MY SOPHOMORE YEAR - ISU 1969-'70

To reach my goals, I knew I needed patience and a lot of hard work with a steady focus on my goal to be a contributing member of a national championship team.

During the spring of my freshman year, freestyle practice in the Iowa State wrestling room was on our own. No coach was permitted to guide or motivate us. Tom Peckham and our team captain, Dan Gable, led the way. I soon realized it was only the hungry few who kept the 3:30 - 5:00 p.m. practices alive in the spring.

The U.S. National Freestyle Tournament that spring was held in Waterloo, Iowa, about 100 miles from Ames. This was close enough for me to get a ride from an upperclassman. I did not place in the tournament, but I competed well enough to receive some compliments and get encouragement from upperclassmen who knew something about Olympic freestyle wrestling.

That summer, Dad found a roofing job for John and me back home. The two of us had plenty of time to talk as we worked together in the hot summer sun. Often we talked about wrestling. Three nights a week we would lift weights and run for conditioning. Again, as we trained, our conversation was often about wrestling. Of course, we wrestled some too. We used an old horsehair mat borrowed from our high school for our wrestling sessions, with a birch tree nearby for shade.

That summer was not just vacation time for John or for me. I was working hard to earn a spot on the Iowa State wrestling lineup, and John was preparing for his junior year at UW Stout. Brother

Dan was still a Cumberland High School wrestler and football player. The three of us trained hard together, pushing each other on every weight we lifted, every step we ran, and every wrestling move or drill we practiced. Each of us wanted to improve as we prepared to meet our expectations for the next season.

Summer Motto

Early that summer, Phil talked with me about making the Iowa State team and actually wrestling for the Cyclones. Checking my self-confidence, he asked me about making the team at 177 pounds. I told him that would be highly unlikely because Chuck Jean was at that weight and would be the returning national champion whom I was not prepared to beat.

"Well, Ben, what about going down to 167 pounds?" Phil asked. I reminded him that Jason Smith was at that weight and was a returning national champion also, and I could not beat him either!

Then Phil asked me, "What about going down to 158 pounds?" I replied that no way could I do that unless I cut off one of my legs, and even if I did, Iowa State already had Dave Martin, a returning second place finisher in the nationals. I couldn't beat him either.

Finally, Phil asked me, "Well then, Ben, what about 190 pounds? Who are the possibilities for Iowa State at that weight?"

I told him All-American Jim Duschen, who was at 191 pounds, had now graduated. (Between my freshman and sophomore years, the NCAA changed the weight classes for college wrestling: 190 pounds replaced the current 191 pound class.) I told Phil that Don Gillespie was likely the top returning prospect at 190 pounds. I would need to beat him in tryout matches if I was to wrestle that weight the next season.

The next day we found a new message written in big bold letters at the top of the blackboard in our basement weight room. It read, "Beat the Great Gadsby." It was Phil's handwriting.

John kidded me about working to beat the Great Gadsby. When I tried to get Phil to change the name to "Gillespie," he just looked at me with a blank stare and ignored my request. So the slogan "Beat the Great Gadsby" stayed on our blackboard all that summer. I knew exactly who it referred to every time I lifted. I was training to beat Don Gillespie in the tryouts coming up that fall.

Sometime later, Dan Gable overheard John and me talking about "Beat the Great Gadsby." Dan asked if I knew what Don Gillespie had done all summer. I replied, "I have no idea." Dan told me that Don was so confident of making the team that he flew to Hawaii and drove a taxicab and had a "good time" all summer. Meanwhile, I was at home in Comstock lifting hard three evenings a week to "Beat the Great Gadsby."

Some wonder why Phil chose the name "Great Gadsby" for our blackboard. Of course, a similarly spelled name, "Great Gatsby," appears in F. Scott Fitzgerald's book *The Great Gatsby*. But to me, "Beat the Great Gadsby" meant much more than just a character's name in a classic work of fiction.

When Phil wrote "Beat the Great Gadsby," it was probably just a play on words, which he always seemed to enjoy doing. It also may have been done to focus my attention not only on my likely opponent Don Gillespie, but also on anyone else I might have to wrestle to make the team.

Regardless of the real explanation, I know this off-season motivation worked! I had a summer motto that gave me focus for my training. It got me ready to work hard and ready to compete at my best in the fall.

Winning a Spot on the Iowa State Team

Returning to campus in September, I resumed daily workouts with my teammates. I was bigger, stronger, and better conditioned than I had been the year before. Now I was really ready to compete for a spot on our varsity team. I still was not picturing myself winning a national championship like some of my teammates, however. Mostly I was focused on earning a spot on the team. The higher focus would come later.

The long-awaited tryout for the 190 pound varsity position arrived and it came down to Gillespie and me. We had four or five tryout matches between us, one every two or three weeks. I won each of them, some by a close score.

In late January or early February, Coach Nichols announced that we would have another tryout match between us. But before we were to wrestle, Don came to me in the locker room and told me he was not challenging me anymore. The starting spot at 190 pounds was mine! I had indeed beaten the "Great Gadsby" and was now a member of the top-ranked college team in America.

But two questions still remained: could I keep the 190 pound spot, and could I contribute to Iowa State winning as a team?

Wrestling Varsity

At the first annual ISU Invitational Wrestling Tournament, which opened our competitive season, I won all three of my matches. As a young wrestler, this was an enormous boost to my self-confidence. Then, on an early season trip to New Mexico and Arizona, I earned some dual-meet wins.

But then it was back to reality. I lost badly in the annual Midlands Tournament in Chicago over the holidays. I found out no one would "roll over" just because I wore the Iowa State uniform. In the Midlands I wrestled Russ Hellickson, a senior at the University of Wisconsin. Russ beat me soundly 6-2 in the second round. But more than just beating me, he really out-muscled, out-conditioned, and just plain out-wrestled me. He left me exhausted.

Coach Anderson later recalled my words as I walked off the mat and he also described his thoughts about me. He relates, "When Ben came off the mat, he said, 'I'm sorry I embarrassed you. That will never happen again.' **That's when I knew he had the heart of a champion, because champions don't like to be embarrassed."**

My Low Point in College

A week later, Bob Underwood of Southern Illinois University pinned me at home in front of an Iowa State crowd. While I was on top riding him with a leg ride I did not arch my back. He simply pulled me over and pinned me.

Beyond any doubt, this was the lowest point in my college wrestling career. It was a sellout crowd that night and most fans were there to watch Dan Gable in his final college season. Most of my teammates won big. My loss by a pin hit me like a ton of bricks. Thoughts of being the weakest link on our team went through my mind. Additionally, I knew that all five wrestlers immediately below me in our lineup could beat me in practice. If it had been possible, I would have crawled under the mat.

A teammate saw me struggling to even finish my shower after the meet and went to Coach Anderson to ask him to come back into the locker room and help me deal with my loss. I will never forget what Coach said to me. In his deep but gentle voice, he did not talk to me at all about my mistakes that night. Rather, he talked to me about my strengths as a wrestler. He assured me I could take people down and that I had proven I could score points against good competitors. He urged me to wrestle more aggressively. I learned an important lesson that night from Coach Anderson; *measure yourself by how high you have climbed, not by how low you have fallen!*

Knowing college wrestling as I do now, I am sure Coach Nichols and Coach Anderson must have discussed my future on the team. But they still encouraged me. And while I continued to wrestle at 190 for most dual meets, I was kept out of the lineup when our lower weight wrestlers were moved up to match up better with an opposing team or to give some of our lighter wrestlers a break from cutting weight.

Two Big Dual Meets with Oklahoma State

The match against Oklahoma State was in Stillwater, and our coaches decided to move much of our team up one weight class. This meant I was out of the lineup and did not make the trip. To be honest, I was a bit relieved not to make that trip. I needed to put the intensity of our wrestling schedule and the demands of my academic studies into better balance. A two-day trip would have added more stress that I would have struggled to handle at the time.

Our team members packed their bags and left. Flying into Tulsa, they arrived in the midst of an ice storm that left the roads covered with solid ice. Traveling in rental cars, they began creeping along the 65 miles from Tulsa to Stillwater. What is normally an hour's drive turned into several hours of stress and a late arrival to weigh in. Nothing at all was normal about that trip.

The next day I heard nothing about our team's goal to win the national championship. Instead, I heard we had lost 13-22. I heard rumors of bad officiating. I heard about weigh-ins that went unsupervised. And I learned that we had been greatly embarrassed.

By practice time the next day, the team had returned to Ames. No one said a word about the meet. No coach commented about it.

No wrestler tried to explain it. And there were no questions from those of us who had stayed home.

There was a stern, determined look in everyone's eyes that day. It was a look that said: "We made some mistakes; we weren't ready; we've been embarrassed. Now let's get to work and never let it happen again." And so, we all went back to work that day more determined than ever. As a young wrestler learning how to compete at the highest level of college wrestling, all this was a great lesson. The resolve of our team completely overwhelmed the natural tendency to back off and recuperate after such a stressful experience.

Hard work cannot change the past after a disappointing performance, but it sure does a good job of changing the future!

Perhaps our most important dual meet that year came in mid-February at home, and it, too, was against Oklahoma State. For that meet, everyone was at his normal weight. At 190 pounds, I was matched up against Geoff Baum, who was undefeated and ranked number one in the nation. Geoff beat me 3-2, and our team lost 17-16.

I was part of college wrestling at its best, but I still failed to score any points for our team in a tight dual meet. On the one hand, I was disappointed with my loss. However, I also knew that I was getting better after going toe to toe with the top-ranked wrestler in my weight class. I had even more reason to keep working hard day after day.

Big Eight Conference Tournament

The Big Eight's that year is a day to remember. I won my first two matches, moving on to meet Geoff Baum. He and I were wrestling in the finals for the conference championship. He was still undefeated and still ranked number one.

The match began with no scoring in the first period. That was a mistake by Geoff. In the second period, I started on top, riding hard, controlling him, and looking for nearfall points. To control him, I used a cross-body leg ride, a near-wrist ride, and an arm-bar ride. Those three rides had become my preferred way to control, wear down, and occasionally turn an opponent. But would they work now against the best wrestler in the nation at my weight?

For the entire second period I rode Geoff without scoring. I would be in the down position to start the third period, and was still fresh while Geoff was worn out from me riding him so aggressively and so long. With quick wrist control and an extension roll, I put him on his back for a two-point reversal and a two-point near fall. Then I worked for still more riding time which, with some pinning attempts, gave me 5½ minutes of total riding time and two more points. I beat Geoff that day by a final score of 6-0 and earned my first conference championship.

My teammates went crazy! I had not lost, and I had not just barely won either. I had dominated in the Big Eight finals against the undefeated, number-one wrestler at 190 pounds. My confidence grew greatly!

Nationals 1970

The NCAA National Championships were held two weeks later at Northwestern University in Evanston, Illinois.

At my weight class the question was; who would be seeded #1? At the seeding meeting the coaches discussed this question. Some argued that since Geoff Baum had just lost in the conference tournament, he should not be seeded first. They argued that others should be considered for the #1 seed. Harold Nichols just listened to the other coaches at first. Then he suggested that I should be seeded #1 because, just two weeks earlier, I was the one who had beaten Geoff so soundly. After still more discussion, the coaches voted: I was seeded #1, and Geoff was seeded #2.

Pleased that he had learned these seeding details, an Iowa State teammate informed me about all this later. I was stunned by my #1 seed.

I did not think of myself yet as a national #1 seed. Rather, I thought that if a top seed were ever to come my way, it would come only after I had wrestled more and won the right to that top seed out on the mat in actual competition. Feelings of enormous pressure plagued me because I still could not forget my early season losses. How could just one victory so late in the season erase those?

In the first round I beat unseeded Scott Christie of Lehigh University 5-0. In the second round I faced 8th seeded Bob Rust of Syracuse University. Rust beat me, just like Hellickson had beaten me earlier in the season at the Midlands. Rust took me down and rode me hard, wearing me out, and leaving me exhausted. He won 6-2. Now the question remained; could I, in spite of my second-round loss, still help my team win the team championship?

To do that, I would have to go through the long wrestleback challenge. I was told: "Take a deep breath and then go to work." Wrestling my way back took four rounds. I won the first three matches 10-0, 4-0, and by default. But I lost my final wrestleback match to #3 seed Jack Zindel of Michigan State. The final score was 0-0, and I lost in overtime on a referee's decision.

Our Cyclone team won the national championship again, and I finished 4th at 190 pounds as a sophomore. I was glad to have played a role in our team's success.

Phil Parker placed third at 134, and four of our teammates made it to the finals. Dave Martin won the championship at 158 pounds, Jason Smith at 167 pounds, and Chuck Jean at 177 pounds. This was the second consecutive national championship for Jason and Chuck.

Through the years, some fans have said this 1970 Iowa State team may have been among the best college wrestling teams of all time. There have been some great teams of course, so for anyone to say we were among the best is a significant compliment.

A tough part of the national tournament was watching Geoff Baum win so easily when he beat Bob Rust 9-1 in the finals. Despite the disappointment, I knew more than ever what it would take for me to win the tournament next year after having just wrestled in it. Twelve more months of hard training could put me on top.

Looking back on my sophomore season, my confidence and motivation greatly increased from the beginning to the end. After the season ended I thought, "I've soundly beaten Geoff Baum, who then easily wins it all! Next year, I can win an individual national championship for my team!" I concluded another year of hard work would make me more consistent and ready to win.

Back to the Basement

As John and I met at home for a summer of roofing houses and barns we were excited about lifting weights together. John's hopes were high. His team had also done well winning their conference tournament. At least two of his teammates were state champions: Hector Cruz and Dale Evans. John was encouraged that he was winning right alongside these two men who had won what John had failed at earlier. Continued work would permit him to keep winning with them and more. He was building way past state level wrestling and he knew it.

Brother Dan was doing well as a junior in high school. His football and wrestling wins were significant. He won everything until he got to state. His sights were set on a state championship.

Phil was excited to be switching to a pulling guard for the Badgers.

All four of us had reason to be hopeful and we were ready to train harder than we ever had in our basement weight room.

—19—
THE UNBELIEVABLE HAPPENS

In winning the national tournament in 1970, Iowa State scored 99 points. Second place Michigan State scored 80. It was great fun to be a part of that national championship team. But there is another story about that national tournament many wrestling fans still remember. It was totally unexpected and almost unthinkable.

Dan Gable is Stretched

Dan Gable, our teammate and captain, was going for his third NCAA title. His opponent in the finals at 142 pounds was Larry Owings from the University of Washington. It was Phil's first time to see Dan wrestle and I was explaining things to him. As Dan and Owings exchanged early points, I laughed when Owings scored. "It's no problem," I said. "Dan always wins in the end." After all, he had won 181 straight matches in high school and college without a single loss.

They were well into the third period and I was still joking around, assuring Phil that Dan would soon gain full control of the match. Then Owings completed a fireman's carry and grabbed a two-point takedown and a two-point near-fall. Suddenly what had been a close match turned into one Dan could no longer win. While Dan made up some of the difference, he lost the match 13-11.

We were stunned! Dan Gable had lost a wrestling match, just like the rest of us. Dan's loss left us all dazed, almost as if we had not even won the national team championship.

I watched Dan as he stood on the awards stand, quietly standing there with tears in his eyes. For some time his head remained down while the crowd stood and applauded, showing their great respect for all Dan had done over the years. And then he raised his eyes to the crowd, acknowledging their admiration.

Wrestling fans love competition, and they love rivalry: including the occasional upset. But they also respect the great skill of a champion, especially matches that go down to the wire and leave no doubt to the effort and desire of both competitors. There are few more emotionally charged moments than the thunderous applause given two wrestlers as they climb the awards stand after a truly hard-fought match, particularly when a previous champion is beaten in a fierce bout.

Dan was a true champion and had taken wrestling to a new level in America, which is why his loss was so surreal, but the applause so intense.

That night I also saw no matter how hard you work, you might still lose. Dan worked harder than anyone I have ever known. And yet, that did not guarantee him a victory in every match. Of course, being thoroughly prepared can make it more likely you will win, but it does not make victory certain.

This is why we wrestle every match as it is scheduled, even when one of the wrestlers is an overwhelming favorite or an overwhelming underdog. Sometimes "things" happen.

Many times I had heard Dan say, "On any given day, anybody can beat anybody." Now, even for Dan Gable, that seemed true. The unlikely winner, Larry Owings, had beaten the unbeatable Dan Gable.

Our team accepted the team championship trophy that night, yet we all felt like we had lost something important. Dan Gable, our leader, our captain, our teammate, our friend, and often our "coach," had just lost for the first time ever in the last match of his senior year.

The next day, a newspaper quoted Chuck Jean saying, "There's no justice in any of this. Gable works harder than any of us. If I could, I'd gladly give him my individual championship." Chuck always had great respect for Dan. Dan and Chuck often trained together, and when they did, it was intense and physically demanding. Dan had helped Chuck immensely as a wrestler, and Chuck was trying, in the best way he could, to say thank you.

Helping a Champion Who Stumbles

In the days and weeks that followed Dan's loss to Owings, I saw him struggling to deal with it. The day after the tournament, our team drove back to Ames. When we stopped along the way for gas, a couple of guys on our team bought a can of beer and asked Dan if he was interested. I had seen Dan say no to this many times before, but this time he said, "Well, since I can't win when I don't, I guess I will."

As the days passed I could see Dan was really hurting from his loss, even when he tried to say otherwise.

After a few days, we continued our training. Although Dan was a senior, he still joined us for freestyle practices and he seemed to be adjusting. Only later would I learn in a class on counselling the steps Dan, and anyone who experiences significant loss, would need to deal with:

Step 1: Deny the reality of the loss
Step 2: Think there is no reason to continue
Step 3: See light in the future
Step 4: Move forward and find new purpose and goals.

The time Dan spent dealing with each of these steps varied. Sometimes the steps overlapped, but Dan was on what was for him a new journey, one that he had not traveled as a wrestler.

Dan was a good friend and great teammate. We all wanted to help him any way we could. I sensed he was battling alcohol and maybe much more. He was not as focused as he always had been, but he was trying hard to get that same focus back.

I wanted to help him, yet I had little idea how God might make me an encouragement to Dan. All this was new for me because, until now, Dan had been the one helping me.

Dan had been a great help over the previous two years just by regularly training with me. He had become not only my teammate, but a friend as well. So how could I best help him now?

That spring, Dan and I had an informal habit of training together each Saturday morning in the Beyer Hall practice room. One Saturday morning I finished my workout; but Dan had not come that day. I did not think much about it because he often had other obligations that could easily have taken him away. Or maybe he had gone home to Waterloo for the weekend. So I really did not think much of it.

After finishing my shower, I began walking toward the athletic training table where I ate lunch and supper every day. It was a long mile walk each way but well worth it because the food there was the best anywhere and I was always trying to keep my weight up. I headed to lunch down one of the two routes available and was walking fast so I would not be late. After crossing Lincoln Way near the campus, I continued up a hill to the next corner. As I entered the intersection, I was preoccupied and in a hurry. Dan came up from my left on a motorcycle. He saw me first, and I did not see him until after he got my attention. He stammered a bit making an apology, but I did not understand why he was apologizing to me. I commented about the motorcycle he was riding. He replied that it belonged to another wrestler who loaned it to him. Then he apologized again, and I still did not know why he kept doing that. Suddenly he got rather intense and said, "I'll bet you were looking for me to practice with this morning. Well, I'll never miss another Saturday practice again as long as I'm in Ames!" With that, we said goodbye and he was off.

It did not make any sense to me why he was so nervous and apologetic that morning. Over the next several weeks I began to piece together what Dan had gone through and what he was likely thinking when we talked in the intersection that Saturday.

The Friday evening before, he had been drinking in the front yard of the house where he and other wrestlers lived. Sometime that night, the Ames police were called to check things out. Apparently, he resisted the police enough that they took him to spend the night in the city jail. It seems Dan spent the night worrying whether the whole state of Iowa might learn about all this.

After he was released in the morning, Dan drove to his campus-area house, going the back way so fewer people would see him. I thank God for allowing me to cross paths with Dan that morning. Of all the intersections in Ames, we both crossed there at the same moment. I still remember his embarrassment. I also remember how that embarrassment changed before my eyes into a renewed resolve that continued undiminished right through the Munich Olympics and Olympic gold.

Even after the Olympics, this same resolve continued. Dan was an incredibly successful head coach at the University of Iowa, winning fifteen NCAA team championships in twenty-one years and affecting countless young men for good. Dan is also an excellent family man. He and his wife, Kathy, have raised four very sharp young ladies.

This experience with Dan reminded me to be sensitive to God's leading. I would not always know to whom, where, when, or how I could help others. However, with God's help, I could always be ready. I especially wanted to help those who had already helped me so much.

By this time in my life, many people had been of help to me. What amazed me that day in Ames was God put me in just the right place at just the right time to help Dan, even though I did not know it and did nothing more than simply be there for a brief conversation.

Later that spring, the National Freestyle Tournament was held in Lincoln, Nebraska. Several of us from Iowa State went to the tournament. It was an excellent tournament for Dan. He won some hard fought matches while Larry Owings lost early without wrestling Dan again. Without all the NCAA fanfare, Dan won a much tougher tournament in Lincoln than the NCAA's.

Although it's true that on one night at the 1970 NCAA National Championships, Owings did what he needed to beat Dan, nearly everyone would agree Dan was a better wrestler than Larry. We all had a satisfying feeling driving home from Nebraska. Dan was a national freestyle champion, and he had proven himself to be significantly ahead of Owings. Two years later at the 1972 Olympic trials, the two men finally met again. Owings failed to give Dan much of a challenge and Dan won 7-1.

Dan's focus had returned and successful wrestling continued to follow.

—20—

FACING TEMPTATIONS WITH GOD'S HELP

Every driven and successful Olympic athlete must overcome many hurdles. As you are probably catching on through the stories about our journey and decisions, there are many lifestyle choices that affect our training and overall health, and therefore our ability to maximize our success.

This chapter deals with sensitive issues. My hope is to share some events that shaped our decisions. And I would like to share a perspective that helped maximize not just our athletic potential, but also the blessing God wants us to be to those we influence.

The first issue is alcohol. It was not brought into our home while I was growing up. When we went to visit Dad's Swedish relatives, we did not see it in their homes either. A total avoidance of the use of alcohol was accepted by most of them so it just never became an issue when I was young.

Mom's family was different. Our contact with her brothers was a learning time for us about the dangers of including alcohol as part of life.

One day while I was working for a neighboring farmer, the farmer's daughter and infant granddaughter were visiting. The farmer and his daughter each had their bottle of beer. They gave me Kool-Aid most likely, and did not push the beer on me. I was underage, an athlete, and they knew my family did not drink. But I groaned as I watched them give the infant a taste of the beer and then laugh when her facial expression showed she did not like it. I was amazed that the infant in a high chair was being laughed into liking the taste of beer.

In high school, I heard stories of classmates trying to impress others by telling drinking stories. I ached for many of them whose families had made it a major part of their lives.

The most blatant stories were told in my high school architectural drawing class. An underage classmate began telling of his experiences at a bar twenty miles away where he and his friends were buying beer. Every time he went, we heard a detailed account of his fighting, vomiting, and hangovers. The more he spoke, the more repulsive it became. I finally asked him not to explain the details to everyone anymore. Desiring to be of help and not judgmental, I asked him if he had considered his future with alcohol. As I started to see even more negative aspects of drinking, I was gaining a total dislike for alcohol along with a desire to help others avoid it.

Growing up in Wisconsin you hear about drinking, and you also hear of alcohol related deaths. I had heard of young people from Cumberland and other neighboring communities who were killed in a drunken accident. It sobered me and again caused me to want to say no to alcohol.

The hippie movement was in full swing when I arrived at Iowa State University. The philosophy being shouted was: "We are free to do what we want;" "All establishment is evil, get rid of it;" "Remove all restraints."

These themes were constantly used as excuses to drink, use drugs, and party. This was especially true on college campuses.

Sound but Sobering Advice

Before I left for Iowa State, my mother warned me of the temptations and distractions I would face. I will never forget the day Mom and Dad brought me to Ames. After getting settled into my dorm room, praying together, and giving each other goodbye hugs, we all walked to the car. As they were getting ready to get in and drive away, Mom told me again that others were at college to simply take classes. She reminded me that I was there also as an athlete and that I would be spending many hours training. Therefore, I could not waste time like many others would.

Mom told me to take every spare minute to review and prepare for class assignments. She also reminded me that I would represent the university in wrestling someday if I kept working and stayed focused. She mentioned that I would be representing the Lord by my life as well. I have never forgotten the way she reminded me of those responsibilities and opportunities. The lesson for me was: use every minute wisely and then enjoy the privileges that come.

Within forty-eight hours, I would be invited to attend the first drinking event. What amazed me was it came from the dorm leaders on my floor of fifty. The upperclassmen felt it their responsibility and privilege to invite twenty or thirty new freshmen to cap off orientation with alcohol. I turned down the opportunity, along with a few others. We had to hitchhike back to campus. I used wrestling as my excuse. With time, I would gain enough confidence to also explain my desire to honor the Lord through the full use of an unaltered state of mind. I had seen immediately that temptations would come from any direction at any time on a college campus.

From the very beginning, I was learning to say no to dorm activities. It seemed every time the dorm unit planned an activity, alcohol was part of it. "Veishea" was a huge carnival-type activity with floats and a parade held in the spring. It was soured from the start with repeated stories of drinking and drunken dorm mates stumbling down the hall at all hours of the night. The float our dorm unit made was clouded with drinking stories. I probably overreacted in some ways, but I was determined not to start drinking. And the best way to do that was to avoid where alcohol was available. So I did not get involved.

Alcohol and Wrestling

As daily fall practices progressed and the team got better acquainted with each other, I began hearing of the drinking done by some of my teammates. At first I did not want to believe that these men with whom I trained, and who very often beat me soundly, were able to break so many of the training rules I had been taught from an early age.

Some of my teammates were the strongest and hardest working men I have ever known. They were fun to be around, friendly, good conversationalists, and anxious to help others whenever possible. We worked out together and developed a definite friendship. But I kept hearing of drinking exploits that were more than the casual one or two beers. I sat on the bench and watched them win match after match until the NCAA team championship was secured. How could this be? Several were way past me in wrestling yet broke the pattern of life I had been taught.

My sophomore year I made the team and began gaining the respect of the other wrestlers. Some kept inviting me to their drinking parties and I kept saying no. They would say, "Ben, you don't have to drink alcohol, you can drink Coke." My response was, "I don't like Coke," (which was true – I never took a liking to it) "but I don't want to go to the party because I know someone will put pressure on me to drink alcohol and I don't want to do that."

One day while discussing the effects of drinking on the lives of wrestlers, one of my teammates told me it was good that I never drank alcohol. He said, "You know, it really tastes bad. You have to learn to like the taste of it." Then he advised me against learning to like its taste. I thanked him for that bit of information and have been thankful my family never tried to make me like it either.

Another day, a couple of teammates saw how much water I was drinking to rehydrate after a hard, hot afternoon practice where I had shed eight to ten pounds. One of them told me, "Ben, it is good you don't drink, because if you ever tried to quench your thirst with alcohol like you do with plain water, you would kill yourself." Again, I was glad my family and so many others taught and exhibited an enjoyable life without alcohol.

When my teammates won the national title my sophomore year it was hard going to the architecture studio. In my classes, we spent considerable time on our own major design projects, yet there was time for us to talk as we worked. I never knew what stories I would hear next about my teammates and their drinking. I was certainly hearing about them in a very different light than I saw in practice. My classmates assumed I did the same things because I was on the team. I began ducking into classes hoping not to get into conversations and wondering what I would hear next.

When one of my teammates killed a deer in a wildlife refuge with a pocket-knife, I knew it was a man controlled by alcohol and not the disciplined wrestler years of training had developed. Our coaches had to go to his aid to help him through that situation.

Then I heard of an incident that became a major issue on campus when one of our wrestlers hit a man over the head with a beer mug. The president of the university got involved and was ready to dismiss him from school. Coach Nichols found another school where the young man could continue his wrestling career, and he was gone in a week. It would be years before I would see him again.

This incident sobered several people, including me, since I had been wondering if the Bible's warnings about strong drink were true. When this story comes up, the following verse comes to mind: *"Do not be deceived, God is not mocked; for whatever a man sows, that will he also reap." Galatians 6:7*

For years people have laughed and joked about all the stories they heard. And for years, I have reminded them of the dismissal of my teammate. My friend could never wrestle in the NCAA's again. He had pulled the rug out from under his career, and an otherwise honest hardworking man's life was significantly altered by a liquid he could not control.

During my junior and senior years, drinking on the ISU team was different. Yes, some did drink and sometimes too much, but they were not excusing it based on the success of others who drank.

The atmosphere on our team changed after some of these instances were publicized. It became easier to speak of my own reasons for not drinking. Most of my teammates and dorm mates figured I avoided alcohol because of my wrestling. But that is not the full story. It was not my central purpose for saying no to alcohol.

It is true that staying sober has been a key factor to my personal wrestling success, and I did not have to fight through some of the obstacles others did. But my greatest motivation has been to please Jesus Christ who loved me enough to die for me, and showed me a way of life that was focused on others rather than fleeting pleasures. During my last two years in college I began to express that belief more openly. I do not think avoiding alcohol makes me better than anyone else. It is simply a way to thank God and let His Spirit have freedom to control me. *"And be not drunk with wine, wherein is excess; but be filled with the Spirit." Ephesians 5:18*

Knowing John and Phil were saying no at their colleges gave me courage to say no as well. John experienced pressure to drink from some of his teammates at Stout. One of them told John, "Before the season is over, it is my goal to get you drunk." Why would a teammate state such a goal?

- Did he think John would be a better wrestler and teammate if he drank to drunkenness?
- Was he looking for an excuse to drink himself?

- Did he think pulling John down to drinking would make himself somehow feel and look better?
- Did he want to see the foolishness of John when alcohol makes a man do foolish things he otherwise would not do?

Maybe there was an element of several, or all, of these in that man's mind, or maybe he was not thinking at all. John and I have discussed this many times, and we have never found a good reason for the man's goal to be fulfilled.

By God's grace, John did not get drunk that season or any other season. He has sought to let the Spirit of God control him instead.

After finishing college, John and I set our sights on the 1972 national team and the Olympics. Again, we faced the joking and occasional mocking from some of the other wrestlers. Even a few coaches questioned us about having an occasional beer. But our reputation was strong and our focus on training preoccupied us at all times. The invitations, jokes, and jabs lessened with time.

One thing that proved disappointing was the perspective of Rick Sanders. Rick was our most experienced wrestler with a silver medal from the 1968 Olympics and a World championship in 1969. Yet stories began to surface that not only alcohol, but drugs were being used and shared with other athletes during the final days before the Munich Games. After the last day of competition, I still remember Rick telling us, "Next year when we get to the training camp, you wake me up to join you in your morning running." John reminded him he would need to go to bed at a proper time the night before to make morning training worthwhile.

What a truly sad commentary. Rick failed to beat the wrestler from Japan and had to settle for silver. The high from alcohol and drugs had taken first place too many nights and Rick wanted to change that. But we never saw Rick again. He was killed in a van accident in Eastern Europe a few weeks after the 1972 Games.

Setting Priorities

Top wrestlers need to make training and competition their major priority. Too often alcohol has taken the primary drive of an athlete. I was learning that strong drink can make a wise man foolish. I saw young men who were considered successful allow their use of alcohol to limit what could have been more successful, and longer lasting, wrestling careers.

Another issue is smoking or chewing tobacco for the "buzz." Just as with drinking, I seldom saw people smoke or chew in my home. Farmers who gathered for fall grain threshing did not smoke or avoided it out of respect when they came in for the meals Mom prepared.

Some of my early memories include a plate as a makeshift ashtray for my mother's brother. We liked it when he brought us fish he had caught. As he sat at the kitchen table and Mom worked at the counter, I gained a glimpse of her heart for her brother. She longed for him to trust Christ for salvation. That may have been my first hearing of the gospel outside of church.

My family, most of the neighboring farmers, and our church family patterned a cleaner way to live and urged me to avoid trying or pursuing that activity. I cannot say tobacco was a serious temptation for me. Very early in life I was turned off by it. As an athlete it was clear from the start it would hinder my conditioning. But I have seen many others struggle with smoking or chewing tobacco and frequently tell me they wish they had never started.

Reaching for Something Higher

I am well aware this chapter may seem judgmental of some of my teammates. In writing this book, I have attempted to show not just the mere facts of our journey, but also the many lessons we learned along the way that helped us reach the success we did.

You will find yourself befriending people whose individual habits you will strongly disagree with and want to avoid, just like we did. This is part of life. When someone accepts and promotes something that can harm us, we must strongly say "no," and at times oppose them.

At the same time I was learning to oppose my teammates drinking practices, I was developing strong friendships with them and working to build team unity. At times it is hard to make this distinction. Wrestling with the seeming contradiction between loving people and choosing a different path, **I was learning that I could love and enjoy the individual, yet dislike the activity that could harm them, me,**

and others. *"If it is possible, as far as it depends on you, live at peace with everyone." Romans 12:18*

A main goal of my life has been to communicate that I am not better than others. Doing good or saying "no" is not going to bring me to heaven. It also does not guarantee success on the wrestling mat. I simply want to be controlled by the Lord Jesus and His Word and not alcohol or some other drug. I make mistakes just as much as anyone else. But through the grace of God, He still forgives sin. By God's grace I want to live a life that says, "Thank you!"

Surviving Anthropology Class Intact

Last, but far from least, you may encounter uncomfortable difficulty in the classroom or other learning situations where the very foundations of your life are held in question. It is at these turning points that the essence of what you believe may be tested. These crises help you solidify life principles for yourself and your future family. Be prepared, and don't miss it for its significance.

There was one class at Iowa State that caused me great consternation. Anthropology could, and should, have been exciting. I often read about the development of people groups in novels and history books, and I enjoyed hearing about people from other cultures.

So, why the conflict? It came from the professor. He was small in stature, but big in energy and opinions. As he lectured a large assembly hall of students, he ridiculed belief in God and everything about creation. My family's God and our faith in Jesus Christ was laughed at and belittled. The small group leaders, who were graduate assistants, helped make the material more applicable.

I remember reading the textbook, which was big in size and cost, and then not wanting to read my Bible afterwards. A spiritual battle went on in my mind all that term. I'm thankful I kept up with my Bible reading habit. By the end of the term I knew my family, other Christians, and God's Word were more stable and gracious than that instructor. I chose Jesus Christ over him and his false teachings and have never regretted it.

See Appendix A – Set Up the Lines of Defense

—21—
WHEN I QUIT, BUT STILL WON MY JUNIOR YEAR - ISU 1970-'71

Like any aspiring person, every young athlete needs to prepare and improve to reach their potential in life. This was certainly true for me in wrestling. To be successful as a wrestler, particularly in my junior year of college, I needed to prepare diligently. I needed to improve my strength and conditioning and I needed to develop and mature my positioning.

I was right on the edge – right between success on the one hand and failure on the other. Which way would I go? I was where the pressures of competition, the distractions of everyday life, and my expectations would either help me succeed or cause me to fail.

Getting Ready to Wrestle

After defeating Geoff Baum so definitely in the Big Eight tournament the previous year, I knew I could win an NCAA championship. When I beat Geoff, he was the number one ranked wrestler in the nation, and he went on just two weeks later to win the national title. Knowing that I could win, and actually winning on the mat, were not the same thing.

After participating in our spring workouts, lifting weights on my own, and completing my second year of studies, I went home to spend the summer with my family. Another summer of shingling roofs every business day with John gave us many opportunities to talk about our wrestling goals and to encourage one another. John would be a senior at UW Stout in the fall and had one more opportunity to win an NAIA national championship. Even though he had not placed in that tournament, he was eager to lift weights, run sprints, and run longer distances to improve his conditioning so that he could finish his college wrestling career strong.

John and I developed a short weight-room slogan that summer, "Beat the Bum." I wrote it in big letters on the old blackboard in our basement weight room. Every bench press, every deadlift, and every squat I did that summer was done to the rhythm of "Beat the Bum." Geoff was a worthy opponent. He had won an individual national title for Oklahoma State and I respected him for it. But "Beat the Bum" served as a motivating motto for my off-season training.

Our brother, Dan, would be a senior in high school that fall and his goal was to win the Wisconsin State Wrestling Tournament. He was the youngest of us five boys and we all wanted him to do what none of the rest of us had done: win the state tournament. All three of us were motivated to work hard and it was another good summer of working and training together. Although we would wrestle on different teams the next season, we trained together like teammates for three months.

World Class Training

Coach Nichols and Dan Gable arranged for me to train that August with the U.S. National Freestyle Team as it prepared for the 1970 World Championships to be held in Edmonton, Canada. The team's training camp happened to be at the University of Wisconsin Superior, about 100 miles north of Comstock. What a tremendous opportunity for me to meet and train with America's best freestyle wrestlers! I attended the training camp for two weeks. When I left, I knew I had a lot further to go in wrestling, but was encouraged by the camp and learned that I was at least competitive with the nation's best.

John also spent a few days at the camp. He remembers watching U.S. freestylers Wayne Wells, Don Behm, Bobby Douglas, and Dan Gable wrestle off for the U.S. Team. This was a valuable experience for John as he later began competing at that level. At the time he was watching the trials, John's self-confidence as a wrestler was so low that he gave little thought to ever competing at that level himself. No one would have guessed that just two short years later this same John Peterson would represent the United States in the 1972 Munich Olympics. At the training camp in Superior John got in a few workouts, but mostly just watched the top wrestlers. He soaked up more than he could have imagined.

Brother Dan

It is always good to hear positive news from home. Dan was in his senior season of football as a running back.

One particular game stands out to Dan yet today. Rice Lake was by far the biggest school in the Conference. It was tough to ever outdo them. But that fall, Dan ran the ball most of the plays in a 45-degree steady rain. No passing, just running plays. Dan scored all three touchdowns in the 18-0 victory.

Coach DiSalvo was ecstatic! Dan recalls him dancing in the center of the field, his suit drenched. After no victories my senior year, I knew Dan, Coach DiSalvo, and his team had put in the effort to make a difference.

Dan would qualify for the state tournament, but competed while sick with a serious virus and did not place. But his athletic success and abilities would get him to NIACC (Northern Iowa Area Community College) where he would play football and wrestle on their national championship wrestling team. After two years, he moved on to wrestle for the Iowa State Cyclones.

John's Expectations Grow, then Crash

When asked what particular wrestling match stands out as a real turning point for him, John says it was the match in the finals of the Midlands Tournament his senior year in college. In the semifinals at 167 pounds, John beat my Iowa State teammate Keith Abens by a score of 4-2. In the finals, John lost to Jim Tanniehill for the third time. Jim was a tough NAIA wrestler who was training to be a national contender in Greco-Roman. Earlier in John's college years, Jim had soundly beaten him in the dual meet between UW-Stout and Winona State University in Minnesota.

But now in the finals of the Midlands, John took Jim into overtime, losing in a close match 3-2. The loss hurt, but John knew he had made it all the way to the finals in one of the toughest wrestling tournaments in the country. And he knew he had lost by the slimmest of margins. For the first time, John was beginning to see that he was actually capable of competing at wrestling's highest level.

Beginning in his sophomore year at Stout, John's goal each year was to win an NAIA national championship. John was an individual conference champion in the Wisconsin State University Conference three years in a row and voted Outstanding Wrestler his senior season. So winning an NAIA championship was a reasonable goal for him. But as a college senior, he was disappointed when he finished fifth at the nationals.

Just as with his losses in the sectional tournament in high school, the sting of losing at nationals really hurt John. He remembers wandering alone on the football field at Appalachian State in North Carolina where the tournament was, crying his heart out after his disappointing finish.

He says, "What added to the disappointment was the fact that Gable had asked me to call and let him know how I had done. How was I going to explain I had taken only 5th in the smaller college division?"

John knows God used that loss to remind him there are far more important things in life than just reaching wrestling goals. He took that opportunity to renew his commitment to other areas of life that needed his investment as well.

Occasionally we would write and keep each other posted on our progress and other happenings. This communication served to strengthen the bond we shared between us. In a postcard, John relayed the results of the nationals and, yet, voiced confidence in me while struggling with his own.

Dear Ben,

We got back this morning at 4:00, traveling through some beautiful country.

Thank you for the inspiring letter Ben. I fished again. Got fifth place, lost in the semifinals. I haven't heard how you did in the Regional tournament but I'm sure you tore everyone apart.

I will be thinking of you for the next two weeks.

John

Back at Iowa State

I returned to Iowa State in September, resuming my daily routine of classes and hard wrestling workouts. By November, my teammates and I were working together again as a complete team. Carl Adams and I were chosen as team co-captains. We were both juniors and had high goals for the team.

My selection as a co-captain and my own expectations motivated me to train extra hard every day. Coach Nichols, Coach Anderson, and our new graduate assistant Dan Gable created a great atmosphere for our young team. We had no returning individual NCAA champions as we did the two years before, and we had no standout seniors. Could we beat the two Oklahoma schools again? Or was our success of the last two years short-lived? I wondered about this as the season began.

As the season progressed, I knew I must be particularly ready for the two dual meets in which I would face Geoff Baum. I also knew I would likely face him in the Big Eight conference and again at nationals.

But first I wrestled Russ Hellickson again in the Midlands. Russ, my fellow Wisconsin native, had now graduated from college and was training for freestyle competition. Russ beat me again in the finals. I was disappointed with my loss, of course, but at least this time I was competitive. The final score was 5-4.

Battling the Baum

This year our team had seventeen dual meets and we won all seventeen of them. Two of those wins were against Oklahoma State. Having trained all summer to the drumbeat "Beat the Bum," my first chance to make good on that training came at OSU. I got a comfortable lead on Geoff early in the match and thought I had stuffed him in a box. However, he managed to chase me the remainder of the match and came within one point. I was irked with myself for getting an early lead and then letting him out of the box. I won the match 7-6.

At home in Ames, it was close again against Geoff and I won 3-2. I was now undefeated in college competition and ranked number one in the nation.

Arriving early to the Nebraska Field House in Lincoln for the Big Eight Conference Tournament, my teammates and I went first to the locker room to check our weight and have a short workout. I was so lost in my own thoughts that I walked right past an Oklahoma State wrestler bundled up in sweat clothes running laps in the hot training room.

When we got to the locker room, one of my teammates asked, "Ben, did you see who that was?!"

I responded, "Who are you talking about?"

My teammate said, "That guy running with all the Okie sweats on. That's Geoff Baum! I'll bet he's cutting to go down to 177."

I could not believe it! After some investigation, our coaches confirmed that, indeed, Geoff was going down to 177. I had never even thought of that as a possibility! For a moment, I was rattled. My goal for a full year was to "Beat the Bum." I instantly felt a mixture of disappointment and relief. Right now, however, I knew I had to refocus on the other quality wrestlers in my weight class, especially those I had not wrestled yet.

Winning the 190 pound weight class at the Big Eight's was easier for me that year without Geoff in the field and I was happy with my accomplishment. Our team finished a disappointing second behind Oklahoma State.

During the final days before the NCAA Championships, I received several letters from my family that were instrumental in helping my mindset. Mom wrote a three-page letter that included these encouraging remarks:

Well, I suppose we should mention your sideline at ISU. How is that getting along - your studies I mean!?! Do you get all your work done? You have a big program, but you are a big man so I am sure you are carrying on accomplishing the necessary requirements.

Dan said he saw in the last wrestling news that you are a national figure! Who would have ever thought that little Ben would ever climb to that lofty height and then keep right on climbing?

Nationals without Geoff

While my teammates and I flew to Auburn University in Auburn, Alabama for the 1971 nationals, Phil drove down in his 1970

Volkswagen Beetle bringing Dad, Mom, and Becky. For many years afterward, they talked about that trip. It was a long, hard drive going 1,200 miles each way with four adults who were not accustomed to sitting all day in a VW bug! But my family greatly encouraged me by being there.

The nationals started well. I won my first four matches by 5-1 over Mike Fiorini of Illinois State, 15-1 over Ted Madden of Princeton University, a pin in 4:49 over fifth-seeded Dave Ciolek of Michigan State, and a pin in 6:14 over Tom Hutchinson of Lehigh. This put me in the finals on Saturday night.

An incidental point, but perhaps of interest to some, is Ted Madden of Princeton defeated Rich Hinebaugh of the Air Force Academy 6-3 in the first round. If Rich had won that match, he and I would have met once again in the second round. As I described earlier, Rich pinned me twice in the Wisconsin High School State Tournament.

After I won my first two matches and Rich had lost, we enjoyed a friendly conversation. I suppose I had nervously wanted to wrestle Rich again. He complimented me on my wrestling and said that although he would have liked to wrestle me again, he stated that I "had progressed as a wrestler far beyond our high school days." That was a great compliment from Rich, my chief rival in high school, and it really encouraged me.

As I watched the other finals matches before wrestling my own, I saw Carl Adams win the national championship at 158 pounds by a dominating score of 18-5. It is always great to see a teammate win! I also watched Geoff Baum win his second national championship: this time at 177 pounds. In the finals he defeated my freshman teammate, Al Nacin, 10-3.

Al often reminds me that he could have been a national champion as a freshman if I had not beaten Geoff and coaxed him down a weight. But Al would do alright, becoming a four time All-American and a national champion at 190 his senior season.

My 1971 Nationals Finals Match

Finally it was my turn to wrestle in the finals. My opponent was 3rd seed Vince Paolano of Syracuse University. After a scoreless first period, we traded reversals in the second period. The pace of the match was fast. Vince was strong, explosive, and flexible. After I got another hard-fought reversal in the third period, I was on top and ahead 4-2. I planned to ride him hard, get riding time while wearing him down, and then turn him for back points. That had been my plan of attack in many of my matches all season long.

But Vince was not easy for me to control with my near-wrist, arm-bar, and cross-body rides. Midway through the third period, he reversed me and showed me his own riding ability. The pace of the match was just too fast for me. My lungs were burning and my stomach ached from nervousness. In the pain and fatigue, I put my head down on the mat and grabbed his wrist just to try and contain his motion. My main thought was I could not allow him to break me down to the mat because that would hurt even more.

All of a sudden I felt intense pain and I gave in to it. I told myself as clearly as if I had said it out loud, “Ben, you’re going to lose this match. You can’t keep going at this pace. It’s just too fast for you. You hurt too much to explode for an escape, so you’re going to lose the match!” My lungs and my conditioning had both failed me. And now my mind also admitted defeat. Was there any reserve at all for me to call on? How could I win now when I had already given up?

Hunkering down under the pressure of Vince’s ride, I slowed way down to ease the pain. While keeping wrist control, I prepared for the end of the match and my approaching loss. What else could I do? After all, I had already given up!

But it was in that moment that the many hours of hard training kicked in. Just surviving day after day for three years against the upperclassmen in the Iowa State practice room, plus all my serious summer weight training, the miles, the sprints, and the long talks with John while we worked as roofers in the hot summer sun were about to pay off. Could any of this help me now? Physically, I was just barely hanging on. Mentally, I was practically beaten.

Then an angle developed between Vince’s body and mine and I felt an opening for a roll. Controlling his right wrist, I twisted to my left and extended my legs, throwing him to the mat on the right. Keeping his wrist, I turned into his hips. This first got me a reversal, and then it got me a two-point near fall. Now I was leading Vince by a score of 8-4. With a couple more scrambling exchanges, the match ended with the final score 11-6. I had won!

After all that angst and uncertainty, I became the 1971 NCAA champion at 190. Standing on top of the victory stand, I thought of the fierce wrestling battle Vince and I had just fought. My stomach was still so knotted up I could neither stand up straight nor smile. In the official NCAA picture taken of the 190-pound place winners, I had more of a grimace on my face than a smile.

Often I have thought about that finals match against Vince. I pretty much quit, yet I still won. How? There were several factors. Vince was just as tired as I was and the pace was too fast for him as well. He, too, was struggling to keep going at breakneck speed. I would wrestle Vince again, and we would hit a fast pace and high fatigue levels before I could beat him. I had trained to fatigue opponents with fast flurries. But I was also learning I might not have enough endurance to complete a match to a victory if I worked my own body too hard and did not contain my opponent. Vince was a great competitor and he stretched me to a new level of intensity and endurance.

Whenever you feel the pace of a match is too fast for you, slow things down a bit while keeping yourself in a fundamentally sound wrestling position and maintain the best pace you can sustain. If you realize you cannot keep up a constant, strong, aggressive attack, adjust to a slower, more stable pace you can manage while still looking for openings.

If you have prepared well and are wrestling an equal opponent, he will be tired too. The winner will likely be the one who can hold solid position and still keep the mind ready when opportunities appear. This was an important lesson for me to learn and remember in my future wrestling. I needed to keep hope alive while waiting for opportunities to develop.

The nationals ended that year with Carl Adams and me winning individual championships for Iowa State. But we were disappointed that the team finished second, far behind our archrival Oklahoma State. We lost that year by 28 points: 94-66. Our second place finish motivated us as we worked to prepare ourselves and our younger teammates for our senior wrestling season.

A Miserable Championship

I tell this story frequently whenever I am out speaking. I consider the next couple months after winning the NCAA championship to be the most miserable time of my life. Most of us are never taught how to deal with success and how to put it in perspective. The lessons I learned during this time were life-changing.

Upon returning to campus, I began having definite stress over the whole NCAA championship experience. So many compliments came about me being the best 190 pound wrestler in America. Maybe my misery was caused by having almost quit and failed, or maybe it was the stress of closure and catching up from all the time missed. And maybe I was over-exaggerating my expectations of winning such an event.

But I became frustrated that since I was such a great wrestler (or so I kept hearing), why was life still full of pressures and why was I no different in dealing with them? In retrospect, I was expecting the national championship to change ME. But my shyness with people was still the same, teachers still required us to learn and complete our class requirements, and architectural design projects were still big every spring. Sure, I was gaining new confidence over time, but I had started to expect, and even hope, that winning such a big event would change my life all at once.

It all came to a head one Sunday morning. Listening to Pastor Brown's message reminded me of the reality that I still had my sin nature. Jesus Christ had still died for me. The truth of the Gospel was refreshing and encouraging to me that day. Christ is the one who cleansed me from sin and changed my heart through His Spirit.

After speaking briefly with Pastor, I recall praying with one of the men. My prayer went something like this, "Lord, I know only You can change me, not winning a national championship. Today, I give that award, that title to you. I don't want to hoard attention for myself. It is yours!"

I walked away encouraged and at peace. Faithful preaching of God's Word had made me see reality. I could not expect a national championship or any other victory to take the place of God and His Word in my life. This would be reinforced many times as each new victory or award required confirmation of my decision to look to Christ for fulfillment and to honor Him with each victory.

—22—

LOVE IS PATIENT

Relationships with the opposite gender can have a significant influence in a wrestler's life. John and I have often thanked God for our parents and the committed, loving example they lived before us. We seldom questioned their love for each other even when things were difficult. When life was hard they did not blow up at each other with words they would later regret. They patiently worked through the tough situations and made a big deal of the positives.

They urged us to follow Biblical examples of purity and commitment to one young lady for life. Scripture not only tells of positive marriages and family relationships, men of the Bible are shown in both their good and bad choices and there is much to learn from each example. In light of this, I began desiring to have a relationship that was positive: the kind I saw shared by my parents and certain marriage partners in the Bible.

After I trusted Christ as my Savior in junior high, I knew the young lady I chose would also need to be a believer and follower of Jesus. This limited things considerably.

As high school started, sports became a primary focus. Though I spoke with several girls, they were simply acquaintances and friends. During my junior year I was attracted to one of the cheerleaders and showed enough interest to walk with her to class for several days. Things were progressing in my mind enough to talk to my mother about her. Mom never told me not to keep seeing her. She just asked if she was a believer and follower of Jesus. When I checked out her family and her direction in life it became quite easy to know what to do. We continued to be friendly, but I stopped meeting her as I had before. I have always appreciated the way Mom gave me a couple key questions I needed to ask in selecting a mate for life.

An important question came from Mom and Dad's example, from Scripture, and from my first simple attraction, "Will I wait for God's best choice for me?"

Distractions Around Every Corner

Before long, society would provide opportunities for me to come in contact with illicit magazines and movies I knew were not a proper use of sex. I knew God had a better way to eventually enjoy the gift of sex. I could imagine what was wholesome and good, or I could fantasize to the point that an ache in my gut would come. This seemed to be the way God designed my body and mind to warn me when something was not quite right.

In the spring of my senior year of high school I was recruited by the University of Washington while the hippie movement was in full swing on the west coast. One memory of that trip still sobers me.

Around noon I was walking across campus from the athletic facility to the cafeteria where I was to eat lunch with some of their wrestlers when there was a lot of commotion in one area. A few male students were running across the street and heading into a section enclosed by a row of bushes and trees. They were hollering to each other to hurry. As one passed me he urged me to join them. For a moment I thought of doing so, even though I had no idea what they were racing to. My curiosity was aroused by their excitement. But glancing at my watch, I saw time was short to get to the cafeteria, so I hardly broke stride and kept going.

Later at supper the students reviewed the day. A part of this new hippie movement that wanted no restraints was open displays of nudity. One of the wrestlers began to describe the time and place of two ladies doing such a display. As I listened, I realized the place and time he described was right where I had been when all the commotion happened. I have thanked God ever since for the row of bushes and the schedule I needed to keep. I was not ready to be a part of that scene. God kept me from something that would have been an unwelcome and ill-timed distraction in my mind the rest of my life.

I was noticing these kinds of temptations would present themselves frequently on a college campus. But I was also seeing God could and would protect me, even when I did not know He was doing so. It made me want to be sensitive to His leading.

On the flight back to Wisconsin I remember thinking negatively about going to college at Washington for multiple reasons. I thanked the coach and the wrestlers for their hospitality, but I did not want to put myself in that setting again.

Within a few days Coach Harold Nichols called and offered me a partial scholarship and the opportunity to wrestle for Iowa State University. Most certainly, a Midwest campus was more appealing to me at that point.

Mom gave me various motherly warnings and assured me of her love and prayers. I could tell that along with her excitement for my opportunities to study architecture and wrestle, there was a concern and burden in her voice that I would keep trusting the Lord and honoring Him.

The September I became a college sophomore, one of the upper class wrestlers thought he should "educate" me. He saw I was shy and very wrapped up in wrestling and studies. Surely, he thought, I must want to experience more things with young ladies.

One day while walking back from supper with him we went by the basement he was renting. He had a mattress lying in a corner of the fully open basement. As we left and walked back to campus he began to describe bringing a young lady down there, and then started to describe his immorality with her.

I asked him to stop. He said, "Don't you want to enjoy this stuff?" I replied, "Of course I do. But I will wait until I find the special young lady I want to marry and spend my life with."

He replied, "Well yes, but you will miss an awful lot in the meantime." After that I was watchful around that young man. I realized his goals were not the same as mine. My goals were to be able to focus on my studies and wrestling while I waited for a trust-filled and love-filled relationship with one lady.

There would be several more times when my focus and resolve would be tested. At one point a roommate talked about an article in a Playboy magazine he had left in the room. In another instance, several wrestlers offered to share their house where I discovered the closet in my room contained a stack of pornographic magazines. In both cases, my mind was quick to try to rationalize how I could look and temporarily satisfy the entirely natural sexual desires God placed within a man.

At first, protecting my own reputation was my major concern in pushing the material aside. The ache in my gut was letting me know this was not God's designed timing or method for satisfying those desires. As time went on, my motivation became more about honoring God's desires rather than merely protecting my own reputation.

In the first case, I am still thankful to my roommate who was kind enough not to leave that kind of temptation lying around after I requested he not do so. In the second case, I realized the temptation would be overwhelming and always present, so I quickly moved back into the dorm.

In both scenarios I was motivated to avoid the material just as much out of fear for my reputation as for actually honoring what I knew to be God's desires. I felt regret about that at the time. The scale would lean steadily the other way as my personal relationship with God deepened and I learned better ways of reacting to, or avoiding, those temptations and distractions.

Relationship Priorities

During my college senior season my roommate, Charlie, came to me after a match telling me of a young lady who was attracted to me. Charlie explained how she talked a lot about me with other students and said she wanted to meet me. At first I brushed it off, but as Charlie explained her persistence, I agreed to meet her.

Charlie set up a date at the snack shop in the next dorm unit. After a few nervous introductions we ordered ice cream and talked about several things. She asked about my wrestling and I asked about her college major and hometown. We ate our ice cream and she asked more questions. As I told her about my family and our Christian beliefs she changed significantly and then cut me off. As she stood up she said, "I didn't come here to get preached at." Then she turned and left.

I just sat there for a while and thought. I did not want to offend her. She asked for this visit. She was attracted to me and wanted to know about me. Wrestling stories were fine, but my faith in Christ was repulsive to her. That was an eye opener where I learned several important things:

1. I did not want a young lady who was attracted only by my wrestling,
2. I would need to be patient and look for a young lady who understood and agreed with my beliefs in Christ,
3. I would need to work at being more tactful telling of my faith in Christ.

The secretary at my college church and I spent several dates together. We shared similar beliefs regarding Christ and it was refreshing to befriend her. Moving back to Wisconsin after graduation would strain and then end that relationship. But I experienced relating with a young lady who also loved the Lord. I also saw that my wrestling did not have to be the center of the attraction.

This simple, friendly relationship was a stark contrast to the stories of immorality and sexual abuse I heard for four years on campus. It was refreshing to get acquainted with a girl I could trust and relate to. I knew God's best for me was worth waiting for.

Lessons Learned Looking Back

Some may think the temptations I have described were small and insignificant, but they were huge to me. Such matters can seem all consuming if we let them. But when I focused on the Lord and His example there was strength to say no.

I have included these experiences to describe issues that drain a man's emotions and alter his focus. When God sends the ache in your gut or the small voice in your heart, or whatever it is you know He signals with, it's time to listen. He always has something better. I have regretted giving in to questionable things, but I do not regret saying no.

As I look back at my college years, I know I over-reacted in various ways. I put myself in an isolated position in the dorms and did not get very close to others. In my focused determination to succeed in the classroom, on the mats, and in honoring the Lord, I chose to isolate myself too much.

I clearly learned no matter how isolated I was from what others were doing, I still had my own weaknesses to deal with. A balance in doing what is right no matter what and reaching out to befriend others can be a healthier path than some of what I chose.

In the end I graduated from Iowa State desiring to meet a young lady who would love the Lord and desire to honor Him by following His design for her life. I prayed for God to send her my way. It would take five years before that would happen when I met my wife, Jan. God knew we were not ready for each other until then. Either way, the wait was worthwhile and the lessons learned extremely valuable.

See Appendix B - Choosing a Greater Good

—23—

JOHN TAKES THE SCENIC ROUTE TO SUCCESS

There was little in John's high school or college wrestling that showed he was ready to wrestle internationally in the Olympics. John was a good high school wrestler but never qualified for the state tournament. Over the Christmas and New Year's holidays his senior year in college, John finished second in the always tough Midlands Tournament in suburban Chicago. That second place finish gave him high hopes for winning a small college NAIA championship. However, he finished fifth and was greatly disappointed.

John's first chance to train briefly with America's best wrestlers came when he went with me for a weekend to the 1970 U.S. World Team training camp at the University of Wisconsin Superior. Although John mostly watched others train, he met Dan Gable, and they wrestled together some. Later that fall, Gable mentioned to me that to build John's wrestling skills and to bolster his confidence, he really needed to train in a more challenging setting.

Choosing to Train at a Higher Level

During the summer of 1971, after John's college graduation, we worked together again as roofers. I was planning to attend the freestyle training camp in Miami for the Pan Am team and I started asking John to join me. But his decision to go to the camp was a difficult one. Having just finished his college career in disappointment, John had little confidence in himself as an elite wrestler and doubted he should go with me. For weeks, he would respond to my suggestion by saying, "Come on, Ben. Are you crazy?"

On the chance I could still convince him to change his mind I called Doug Blubaugh, coach for the Pan Am team, and asked if John could attend the training camp in Florida. Coach Blubaugh, a 1960 Olympic champion at 160 pounds, was always willing to give an eager young wrestler an opportunity. He told me, "Sure, Ben. If he will work as hard as you do and if he pays his own way to get there, he's welcome to attend."

About a week before I was scheduled to fly to Florida, John and I had one last conversation about whether he should go with me. We talked while we were seated on large farm tractors at Bents Motors in Comstock. Our running routine, which began when we were still training for high school football, was to run the mile to Comstock, take a short break, and then run sprints on the way home. While resting on a tractor, John compared himself negatively with America's best wrestlers and asked again, "Why, Ben? Why should I go? These are the best freestyle wrestlers in America!"

My rather impatient response was, **"John, don't compare yourself with someone else. They may be headed for failure!"**

He thought for a moment and quickly stepped off the tractor. He stood on the side of the road, anxious to start our sprints, and stared at me as if to say "are you going to sit on that tractor all night?!"

I am sure I did not beat him in any of our sprints that night. John had new determination. Only time would tell whether he would actually make an international team and compete for the United States, but John was now committed to give it his best shot!

And with that, he agreed to go. He bought a one-way plane ticket from Minneapolis to Miami. His new determination to take his wrestling to a higher level was tested at the airport ticket counter. As he and I checked in, we learned there was an extra $64 charge he had not anticipated. After a brief hesitation, John concluded: "I've come this far, I'm not turning back now." And with that, he paid the additional fee and we were on our way.

Working Hard at Training Camp

The Pan American team camp brought John to a whole new level. Working daily with Bob Anderson, the number one wrestler in his weight class, with Dan Gable, and other experienced wrestlers enabled John to make enormous strides each day in his technique, conditioning, and self-confidence.

About a week into the Florida camp, I noticed Gable often chose John as his training partner. Although I felt envious standing on the side, I remember thinking, "Get over it, Ben. This is great!" I knew John would develop significantly and he would quickly get better because of his hard training with Dan.

The truth was John had already learned to work hard day after day. Of course he had occasional fears as we all do when our current performance falls short of our expectations. But he knew he wanted to do more than he had done so far, so he kept working, listening, and taking advice every day.

Finding a Way

After a month in Florida of continually drilling his double-leg takedown and polishing his other skills, we flew to the U.S. World Team training camp at the U.S. Naval Academy in Annapolis, Maryland. John believed he was now ready to be competitive in the trials.

A few days before the final team trials began, a pre-camp freestyle tournament was scheduled for those who had not yet qualified through one of the national tournaments. I was already qualified because I had won the NCAA tournament that year. But John had no previous qualification and he needed to wrestle through the pre-camp tournament. Although he showed some promise, he failed to make the roster of those eligible to participate in the final ladder.

Then someone suggested, "John, why don't you try to qualify through the Greco-Roman pre-camp tournament?" After initially objecting to this suggestion because he had never wrestled Greco before, he concluded, "Since I've come this far, why not try it?" After evaluating the weight classes and looking at the number of competitors in each class, an experienced wrestler advised John to wrestle at 220 pounds.

Because of the lack of Greco Roman participants at 220, John placed second in a field of just two, and qualified to attend the World Team freestyle training camp! At the end of his qualifying match, the referee delayed John before he left the mat and jokingly asked him to promise he would never again wrestle in a Greco match. John just smiled back.

Even so, as a top-2 finisher in the Greco tryouts, John was now eligible to compete in the final World Team Freestyle Tournament. You may wonder how he could qualify for freestyle by wrestling Greco. During this era of wrestling, the U.S. Wrestling Federation sponsored the team for a year and encouraged participation in both styles by allowing us to try out for freestyle and Greco.

When the obvious route was blocked, John found another way. By the way, stories like this still happen. In all the hype about how hard it must be to make a national team, many wrestlers just fail to show up. This leaves the field open for those hungry enough to try.

Each of John's tryout matches in the final World Team Mini-Tournament was close right up to the end, but his extraordinary physical conditioning paid off. He did nothing fancy; mainly relentless double leg takedowns. Two of the wrestlers whom he beat had defeated him just the week before in the pre-camp tournament. But John was rapidly improving. Some have said he was improving by the minute.

Something that wasn't an improvement however, was the dye job he and Mom tried to impose on his singlet. John didn't like the white singlet he had so they tried to dye it Packer green. The more it was washed the more it faded to an awkward pea green. J Robinson kids him about it yet.

One of John's opponents was Jack Zindel, who had wrestled and played football at Michigan State University. Two years earlier, Jack had beaten me in overtime on a referee's decision for third place in the NCAA tournament. But this time, Jack lacked the superb conditioning needed to hold off John. Coming from behind, John won the match.

His final match was against Wayne Hicks of the Naval Academy. John beat Wayne with his basic double legs in a low scoring match.

In just one week, John had his hopes dashed, found a back door, and earned his way through an incredibly challenging tournament to make the U.S. team at 180.5 pounds. He was now on his way to the 1971 World Freestyle Championships in Bulgaria!

Everything fell into place almost like a dream for John in making that team. He says, "Much of making a World or Olympic wrestling team is simply being in the right place at the right time."

You can control much of your own training habits, but you have no way to predict or control many other factors in determining your ultimate experience.

I made it through to the finals and faced Russ Hellickson. I have little memory of that match other than he won again. I was so amazed and excited for John's victory that my loss was soon forgotten. John was greatly surprised he made the team and not me.

A Huge Thanks to our Coaches

John had laid the foundation for his success with multiple hours of training. However, many coaches helped prepare John in the early days for this moment in time:

- Coach Joe Hegenbarth, his wrestling instructor in junior high P.E.
- John Rutter and Jack Walsh, his high school coaches
- Henry Yetter, wrestling coach of nearby Amery
- Sten Pierce and Rick Heinzelman, his college coaches at Wisconsin Stout
- Coach Doug Blubaugh, who gave John permission to train with the 1971 Pan American Team.

1971 World Championships

John's experience at the championships in Bulgaria was of great importance to him. Although he did not win any matches, the tournament gave him a sense of what was required of an international wrestler. He also saw Gable win a gold medal. That, in itself, was significant, showing John firsthand that an American can win a World championship.

It is also true John's first international trip did not give him much reason to believe he would represent the United States in freestyle for a major part of the next decade. It gave him little reason to think that the very next summer he could win a medal for the United States in the Olympics.

After the World Championships ended, John lost in several dual meets the U.S. team had scheduled in West Germany. Thinking his trip to Bulgaria may be his last trip to Europe, John stayed for a few extra days in London to do some sightseeing with Coach Ed Perry.

Coach Perry was the head wrestling coach at the U.S. Naval Academy in Annapolis, and he was the team leader for the U.S. team that year. John really enjoyed the extra stay.

An Invitation from Gable

After returning home in September, John called me with a question. "Gable has asked me to come to Ames to train all winter and try to make the U.S. Olympic Team next summer. Ben, what do you think I should do? Should I join Dan and train at Iowa State?"

Dan must have seen serious potential in John, and he must have concluded John would be a good workout partner. My answer went something like this, "Duh, John. That's a no-brainer. Get down here as soon as you can!"

All John's hard work as a wrestler over many years, repeated second and third attempts after earlier failures, listening to and learning from others, and using the opportunities that came his way to train with tougher and tougher wrestlers was now paying off. Gable's repeated words of encouragement to John, together with Gable's actions backing up those words, built John's confidence step-by-step to heights he had never known before. Thank you, Dan Gable! John and I are thankful for your patience in working with us.

Dan's invitation for John to come and train in Ames was the most important factor in John advancing from fifth place in the NAIA nationals to earning a silver medal in the 1972 Olympics.

U.S. Military Service

In the late 1960s and early '70s, graduating from college was stressful for most young men because of the unpopular Vietnam War. After graduation, college deferments ended and men were subject to being drafted into military service. Tom enlisted and Phil was drafted into the Army, and both served at different times in South Korea.

John had a low enough lottery draft number that it seemed likely he would be drafted after graduation. Ironically, when he went for his first military physical exam, he failed it because of his earlier knee operation and his flat feet. When he was called in a few months later for a second physical, John passed the exam. But by then, the war was winding down and fewer soldiers were needed. John was never drafted.

We remain grateful to others, such as University of Minnesota Wrestling Coach J Robinson, who served in Vietnam while John and I were training to make the 1972 Olympic Team. When we are tempted to feel too self-important about our Olympic accomplishments, it is good to remember that many things had to fall into place for us to succeed in the Olympic Games. If others had been given the same training opportunities that were available to us, they may have had Olympic success as well.

I must also add there were frequent prayers for John and me all along our way to the Olympics. Our parents and family, many friends, and John and I prayed for God's direction and His approval in all we did. And God graciously answered those prayers!

—24—

A STILL HIGHER GOAL MY SENIOR YEAR - ISU 1971-'72

After a two-week break following the nationals in March, I began training for my senior wrestling season. During those two weeks I ate well, caught up on sleep, and concentrated on my studies in architecture. By the end of the break, I felt sluggish and lazy. I was eager to get back and have a good hard workout.

Weight training, running, and wrestling freestyle with my teammates were just what I needed. No coaches were necessary, no formal demands, just training because we wanted to and because we wanted to get better. We were simply training because another wrestling season would be here before we knew it.

That spring I learned I would be allowed to go to the U.S. Pan Am training camp in Miami, Florida, and the Senior U.S. World Team training camp in Annapolis, Maryland. I would have an opportunity, at no cost to me, to train for a number of weeks with the best freestyle wrestlers in America.

Summer Training and Wrestling

Arriving home in June 1971, I spent a month and a half roofing houses and barns with John. As I described earlier, it took considerable time and effort to persuade John he should go with me to those two camps. In the end, he agreed to go. As a result, we trained together with America's best freestyle wrestlers for half of the summer.

My long-time Wisconsin rival, Russ Hellickson, won a gold medal that summer in the Pan Am Games. He went on to win a bronze medal in the 1971 World Championships in Bulgaria. According to historical records, Russ's gold and bronze medals were the first international wrestling medals won by a Wisconsin native. Russ showed everyone that Wisconsinites can win at wrestling's highest levels.

After sending John off to Bulgaria, I enjoyed a two-week visit with Mom and Dad back in Comstock. They had just sent Dan off to preseason football practice at North Iowa Area Community College in Mason City, Iowa. Mom fed me very well and we talked a lot. I left home re-energized and eager to get back to Ames for my senior year of studies and my final year of wrestling for Iowa State. I was glad to be back training in the Cyclone room with the hardest working college wrestlers anywhere.

Final Season at Iowa State

Iowa State standouts like Carl Adams, Keith Abens, Rich Binek, and Al Nacin were eager to train hard for a run at the national championship. All of them were great workout partners.

We also had newly crowned World champion Dan Gable in the practice room. Dan was hired for a second season as a graduate assistant. In addition, John came to Ames that fall to train with our team. This was great for John, great for me, and great for our team. Also joining us in the practice room was a mountain of a man: good-natured Chris Taylor. He was 6 feet 5 inches tall, and he weighed about 425 pounds. Yes, that's right, 425 pounds!

Those were the days of unlimited heavyweights, and Chris was one of the biggest heavyweights ever. He would also turn out to be one of the best college heavyweights ever, winning NCAA championships in each of his two years of NCAA wrestling.

I cannot count the number of times people have said, "Ben, you didn't really wrestle Chris, did you?"

Of course I did! Why not? Who else was going to work out with Chris? Most other heavyweights would quit the team rather than try to beat Chris. I was the next biggest wrestler in the practice room, and Chris was an actual mountain to conquer. For a year and a half, I wrestled Chris regularly in practice. And I learned a lot!

I am privileged to have had all these men as my teammates to train with daily for an entire season. Some were already top notch wrestlers while others were working hard to become champions before they graduated. And we all shared the same team goal: beat Oklahoma State and the University of Oklahoma, and win another national championship for Iowa State.

All these wrestlers training hard together every day gave us top quality competition. Harold Nichols and Les Anderson had put together an excellent team. Over thirty wrestlers trained together daily on just 1½ mats. Our practice room had padded walls and was located on the third floor of Beyer Hall. When I see the more spacious practice rooms many colleges have today, I wonder how we did it. Perhaps the limited space just added to our intensity.

When I think back about our practice room, it provided a terrific atmosphere for training championship wrestlers. It brings to mind the words of Scripture: *"As iron sharpens iron, so a man sharpens the countenance of his friend." Proverbs 27:17*

My teammates were the iron that sharpened me, and in turn, I helped sharpen them. Indeed, it was a year for all of us to remember.

Our first competition was at the Southern Open in Chattanooga, Tennessee. With just seven wrestlers entered (including Gable and John), Iowa State won five of the weight classes. We lost only to each other. When we returned to Ames, we learned the rest of our team had won the Northern Open in Madison, Wisconsin. Our wrestling season was off to an excellent start!

The Southern Open was an introduction to traveling and competing alongside Chris Taylor. He and I rode in the same car on the trip back to Ames and had time to get better acquainted. For lunch we stopped to eat at a buffet. On the way back out to the car Chris exclaimed, "Man, Ben! You eat more than I do!" I'll admit I ate some serious chicken that day. Some of the other guys were watching their weight and were conscious of it all the time. Not me! I was conscious of when the next meal was going to appear. Later in the season I agreed with Chris that I could eat as much as he could, I just didn't eat all day. Chris and I became good friends. All of us learned to deal with the attention the media, the fans, and the ordinary person at a buffet gave to Chris. If he was with us, we were the center of attention.

After three dual meets, we were off to Chicago for the Midlands Tournament. In the 190-pound finals, I again wrestled Russ Hellickson. By just the narrowest of margins, I won the match on a referee's decision in overtime. After three tries in the Midlands, I had finally beaten Russ. This was a milestone!

John built his confidence further by beating my teammate, Rich Binek, in the finals of the Southern Open and the Midlands. Rich had been a Junior World champion and would become an NCAA champion.

Gable and John Train and Compete in Tbilisi

Meanwhile, Gable and John were giving all their attention to freestyle. They traveled to the great Tbilisi Tournament held each year in Tbilisi, Georgia, one of the republics of the former Soviet Union. Tbilisi is located far to the south of Moscow in the Caucasus Mountains. The quality of wrestling there is terrific. Traveling to Tbilisi was a great training experience for John and it helped prepare him for the 1972 Olympics.

At the Tbilisi tournament, Dan's good sense of humor was great for John's nervousness. John loved to talk about watching Dan out-wrestle his opponents. Dan was named the "greatest wrestler" in the tournament and received a large cloak for achieving that honor. John remembers walking off the wrestling mat after being pinned by a Soviet wrestler and having Gable immediately ask him if he knew who had just pinned him.

John mumbled, "All the Soviet wrestlers look alike to me."

Dan replied, "John that was Levan Tediashvili, the Georgian. Last summer in Bulgaria, he won the World Championship!"

"Well, Dan, why didn't you tell me that before I wrestled him?" John responded.

With a twinkle in his eye, Dan answered, "I knew you weren't ready!"

Gable knew John was not yet confident enough, so he didn't use that information for motivation. Dan took the responsibility on himself to help John prepare for the next time he would face Levan. A month later that happened in Anoka, Minnesota. This time John lost by only two points. Not a win, but a confidence-builder either way!

Training for College and Beyond

After returning from the Tbilisi Tournament, Dan and John's training pace quickened. Every afternoon after the Iowa State team had finished its regular practice, they would stay longer and go hard for another thirty minutes or more. I wanted to be a part of that, too. So every day we practiced collegiate wrestling with my Iowa State team for an hour and a half, took a five minute break, and then worked on freestyle.

People often ask me how I switched from college wrestling to freestyle so quickly. The answer is simple. I was already wrestling freestyle in the spring and summer, and in my senior year, I wrestled freestyle every day. Adjusting to the differences in the rules and to the greater emphasis on back control in freestyle is hard for many wrestlers. In my mind, I was adjusting to those differences every day. For me, switching from college to freestyle wrestling became as simple as taking off my headgear.

Dan and John were training together in the morning, afternoon, and evening. By mid-February, I saw them moving way ahead of me in freestyle. By then, I was also serious about trying to make the 1972 Olympic Team. I mentioned to Dan that maybe I should sit out the rest of the college wrestling season so that I could concentrate solely on the Olympics coming up that summer.

Dan wisely responded, "Ben, what makes you think you can make the Olympic team if you can't also win the college nationals? Keep your focus on winning in college, and there will be plenty of time for you to get ready for the Olympic Games. Just keep training freestyle with us every day."

That was sound advice from Dan, and I needed it. The college nationals became a stepping stone for me to an even higher goal, Olympic gold. My college training and competing for Iowa State provided a strong "base camp" from which I later would climb the mountain all the way up to the Olympics.

Senior Nationals

Iowa State won seventeen dual meets and lost just one. Chris and I took full responsibility for that loss. At the University of Washington we had few fans in the house compared to the hordes of Washington fans who had turned out "en masse." Chris and I were the last two weights to wrestle and occasionally it came down to us to win it. After several hard fought matches in the lower weights, both Chris and I had to win, and one of us had to pin. I wrestled first and turned the man. I had him on his back more than once but I could not secure the fall. Their fans went crazy every time he got away. Throughout the match I thought, "I want to get this pin, but if I don't, Chris will." He pinned most of his opponents and I was counting on it. I won 10-0, but not by a pin. The Washington fans cheered again. Now it was Chris's turn. His opponent had been well coached to stay off his back and avoid Chris. Chris chased his man throughout the match but was unable to turn him and get the pin. Chris won 8-2. The Washington fans erupted as if their man had won. Even though Chris and I had won individually, we felt like we had lost. After the meet was over, we apologized to each other for not getting the pin. This team loss of 16-17 ended a 2-year winning streak for ISU.

We finished second to Oklahoma State in the Big Eight Conference Tournament and were off to nationals at the University of Maryland in College Park. Carl Adams repeated as the national champion at 158 pounds, Chris Taylor won at heavyweight, and I won again at 190 pounds, giving our team three individual national champions.

We racked up additional team points from others who placed: Bill Fjetland fifth at 126, Phil Parker second at 134, Keith Abens second at 167, and Rich Binek third at 177. As a wrestling team, this was Iowa State's third national team championship during my four years in college. As team co-captains, winning the team title in 1972 was tremendously rewarding for Carl Adams and me.

In the finals, Carl beat Stan Dziedzic of Slippery Rock University 7-4. Chris Taylor beat Greg Wojciechowski of the University of Toledo 6-1. My matches at 190 included pinning John Hohman of New York University in the first round in 2:58, pinning Randy Corn of the University of Washington in 4:03, defeating Kelly Bledsoe of Portland State 5-1, and defeating Greg Strobel of Oregon State 13-1. In the finals I beat Emil Deliere of Princeton by injury default in 1:53. When Emil tried his duck-under I hip tossed him on his back. He tried to continue wrestling but was unable to.

How privileged I was to be part of this Iowa State Cyclone run of national championships. As a team, we gained great momentum my freshman and sophomore years, lost some of it my junior year when we finished second, and regained it in my senior season. I could never have imagined being part of such a winning college wrestling program, nor how the momentum from that Iowa State team would carry some of us forward to even greater wrestling accomplishments after college.

Eight months later, I graduated from Iowa State University with a bachelor's degree in architecture. The words of Scripture describe just how I felt: *"The lines have fallen to me in pleasant places: Yes, I have a good inheritance." Psalm 16:6*

—25—

WRESTLING THE EXTREMES

As a high school wrestler, I often trained with our heavyweight, Ricky Chartraw. Ricky was quite a bit shorter than me, but he was much heavier and a lot stronger. As I would attempt wrestling moves on Ricky or he on me, I became aware of the need to protect myself against injury. Wrestling with Ricky in high school was just a taste of what I faced later in college and Olympic training camps.

As I mentioned earlier, Chris Taylor was one of my Iowa State teammates and again on the '72 Olympic Team. Chris was a big, big man standing at 6' 5" and weighing in at 425 pounds back when there was no weight limit for heavyweights. Facing him on the mat was a whole new challenge. Since I was in the next lower weight class, it was only logical that he and I would often wrestle in practice. I was a team co-captain, so if I offered excuses to avoid working out with Chris, others would certainly do the same. That would not have been good for our team.

When I first wrestled Chris, my immediate reaction was to run away in fear from this larger man. His immense power scared me. I sensed his weight might smother me. I felt helpless, and a feeling of helplessness is never a good thing for a wrestler. It would have been easy to conclude that it was impossible for me ever to stay safely on the mat with Chris Taylor.

Once I got past the initial fear, I learned two things that were very useful:

- Chris was a gentleman, and he was my teammate. He did not want to hurt me. He wanted to learn and improve just as much as I did.
- I needed to learn to deflect the much greater power and

> weight of my far bigger opponent. Patience, foresight, and always maintaining a sound wrestling position were the keys to avoiding injury when facing Chris. I learned first-hand that a bullfighter never charges the bull. Instead, he deflects the bull's charge.

My advice to young wrestlers is to wrestle occasionally in practice against men who are much bigger than you. Begin by taking your time. As you begin to feel comfortable wrestling people your own size, slowly move up to bigger opponents. Study and watch what a bigger man does. If he charges you or if he has spurts of frustration, keep some distance from him and deflect his power. Do not leave yourself unprotected against a bigger, stronger opponent's power and weight. And remember, if you get caught in a vulnerable position, just swallow your pride and beg for mercy. Then start over again. But always be careful!

If you think the sport of wrestling is only about power and determination, beware! Sooner or later, you will face someone with more power and even more determination than you have. *So always work to establish and maintain a sound position.* This is the most important key to good wrestling. Use your power and your gutsy, gritty determination, but always use it while starting from a proper position.

Wrestlers learn best to keep a sound position by trial and error, by wrestling over and over again from many different positions. You begin to learn which angles work best and which do not. And nothing is better than wrestling a talented larger man to learn what angles work and how to deflect an opponent's superior power and weight.

Practicing with a Smaller, Faster Wrestler

Similarly, I had the great benefit and privilege of regularly practicing with a terrific wrestler who was much smaller and faster. Dan Gable was forty to fifty pounds lighter than me and for nearly four years we wrestled hard with each other several times a week. Dan showed me how to deflect an opponent's power and weight when he would protect himself from my attacks and shift to attack me from another angle. He seldom fought my power or weight head-on. He would deflect it. Since I was heavier and stronger than Dan, it was extremely important for me to understand this need to deflect an opponent's power and weight.

As time passed, I learned to tie up Dan's speed. This is essential for a champion. Sooner or later, you will face someone at your own weight who is faster than you are. When this happens, it is essential to slow your opponent down and tie up his speed. As a heavier wrestler, there is no better way to learn this skill than by working with the men on your team who are lighter and faster. Regularly wrestle your lighter teammates even though they may seem like an annoying, pesky fly.

Wrestling the Extremes

Take your time. Do not rush into training with someone who is much bigger or much smaller than you. Once you have developed patience and basic skills, and can maintain sound position against wrestlers your own size, you can learn some great technique by working with your bigger and smaller teammates.

In addition to improving your wrestling, you may also build some great friendships. Chris Taylor was a good friend until he died in 1979 at the young age of 29. Dan Gable is still a very important friend of mine. I would not have won two NCAA championships without Dan. I would not have won two Olympic medals without Chris. Training with each of them was essential to moving on to a new level of wrestling.

—26—
WORKING THROUGH RACIAL TENSION

Prejudice is a part of human nature. This tendency happens frequently between races and nationalities. I find I need to work against the crude talk of the world and my own tendency to question someone who is different than me.

Growing up in northern Wisconsin I seldom saw a man with black or even dark skin. We were Swedish, Norwegian, German, Italian, and a few Native Americans. I do not recall my parents ever telling a racist joke. They were puzzled and troubled by some of the methods of the racial movement of the '60s, but they never left the impression that any man was inferior or not entitled to the freedoms and opportunities we enjoyed as Americans.

That changed when I entered Iowa State. There were three African Americans on our wrestling team and many more around campus. My first reaction was to test each person for their individual character. Were they someone I could work with, befriend, or spend time with? I was taught to seek what is right, best, and good. If others wanted the same, it was easy to become friends.

Carl Adams was one of these men. By our junior year we were building a good friendship. I saw him as a highly disciplined, hard-working man. He was patient and soft spoken, and he was quick as lightning on the mat. He made the team all four years, building his skills and confidence each year. We were co-captains our junior and senior seasons. We repeatedly discussed how we could get, and keep, all the wrestlers running extra outside of practice.

We won most tournaments our junior and senior years. For two years Carl and I matched records almost perfectly, winning the NCAA championship twice in our respective weights. As a junior, I was named the Iowa State Outstanding Wrestler. Various alumni had endowed this honor, giving a heavy 2-foot long engraved silver tray to the honoree. Carl was named the Outstanding Wrestler our senior year. My wife, Jan, often uses my tray to serve special meals and desserts. When she does, I think of Carl and the friendship we built and the victories we won together. And I think of his family using his tray.

After graduation, I moved to Wisconsin while Carl continued at Iowa State to get his Master's degree and help coach the team. Three years later we made the 1975 World Team together. I urged him to continue his freestyle, believing he could do very well internationally.

After Montreal in 1976, I was gone again and Carl moved to New England where he has coached ever since. Today we chat at tournaments when we cross paths. I always compliment him on the professional image he portrays and the master wrestling technician he has become. Wrestling books, technique videos, and takedown machines are all tools he has developed to help wrestlers. He has patiently continued to work as a coach and people respect him for it. He has always been professional and positive and reminds me to work hard for the same.

The differences and prejudices of life can often hinder relationships. But when men are reasonable and honest, the real character of a man can be proven. Honest and respectful relationships can develop as a result. It is rewarding to build team unity, personal maturity, and friendships with men of diverse backgrounds.

I thank God for friendships that have developed through my involvement with wrestling. And I am thankful for Carl Adams and pray God's best for him. After graduation I trained at Iowa State with Willie and Charlie Gadson. Today, I remember them as men with a great sense of humor, as hard working wrestlers, and also caring gentlemen. Their positive and winsome spirit made many hard workouts fun and memorable. I thank God for these men and for the experiences and learning we enjoyed together.

It took too long for me to build relationships with others while I was in college, including those of other races. With time that has become easier. Unfortunately, learning to break through barriers of awkwardness or misunderstanding takes time, just like learning new wrestling technique takes time.

Today racism still exists in various forms. We find instances that shock and disappoint us and are truly tragic. We need to remember that God made us all in His image (Genesis 1:26).

Treat others with the respect each human deserves and never underestimate the value of simply "being" together. Sports, especially wrestling, have always been a great barrier-buster because sport is a universal language. When unsure what else to do, start a sports conversation - especially on the mat!

I am very thankful for the years of experiences and learning with so many unique and diverse people in the sport of wrestling. These individuals have made the journey more memorable than the journey itself did. Work to make friends while you wrestle and not enemies no matter what the potential prejudice.

—27—

THE VALUE OF SPIRITUAL ENCOURAGERS

Choosing a church family was important to my parents, and eventually to me. When I was three, they decided to drive twenty-one miles to a new church. The strongest message I heard was the fact that my parents showed the importance of the gospel by making that drive to Rice Lake almost every Sunday.

As I grew up, the men in the church became important to me. Some of them were farmers and loggers, while others worked at various businesses. It was a healthy mixture of men and women who understood Christ's sacrificial death for them and who wanted to tell others of that truth.

I still remember with fondness the music they loved, especially the quartet of farmers and loggers. I am no musician, but I know those men exhibited an excitement and joy that I still appreciate in a church family.

John and I recall one farmer who was our Sunday school teacher while we were in middle school. Stan motivated us to memorize scripture and each week he would reward us for what we had learned. The biggest reward was an overnight fishing trip deep in the north woods. We had to walk over a dam to get to the other side of the lake. I was too scared to walk through the rushing water, so Stan carried me over. John still kids me about that. Also while fishing, one of the other boys got a fish hook stuck in his ear. We will never forget that trip or the investment Stan made in us.

I also appreciated Reuben, who worked for the power company. We would often talk together after church. These talks began in high school and continued well after college when I was home for an occasional visit. He would ask about my goals as a student and as an athlete, and then about honoring the Lord. These conversations were memorable because he was interested in me, and he was also genuine about serving the Lord.

When John and I went off to college we looked for a church we could call our own. John still speaks of the church family that had a definite impact on him while at UW-Stout. He still has contact with people there.

My freshman year at Iowa State, I immediately made contact with the Ames Evangelical Free Church. This was the kind of church we attended back home, so it was quite natural for me to attend there. The church itself was relatively new.

A young couple picked me up at my dorm every week. I was encouraged by them and attended for two full years. Then in the spring the pastor resigned to minister in another place. The church continued to have guest speakers into the fall as they looked for their next pastor. I grew anxious for the stability of a permanent pastor.

A college group called Navigators had Bible studies on campus. In the fall of my junior year I attended these studies along with three or four others. I appreciated meeting other students who believed the same things I did. I voiced my frustration that my church was having so many speakers but did not have a pastor. It was also halfway across town which required getting a ride every week. The leader of the study group pointed me to Campus Baptist Church. He stated, "Their building is just two blocks away. You could easily walk there for all the services you want." I listened but I thought, "I have seldom been to a Baptist church, so no need to start now."

Within a couple weeks, I was standing outside my dorm on a Sunday morning waiting for my scheduled ride. After a while, I realized no one was coming. Questions arose: Was I late? Did the couple not come? Should I call the church to have someone come? That other church is two blocks away, should I go there? I decided to give it a try.

That Sunday they had a guest speaker as well. The church experience was okay in my thinking, but the speaker was more forceful than I was used to. Nice people and a good experience, but I thought, "I'll be up early next week to go back to the other church."

The next Sunday, I was up and waiting. Again, no one came.

After waiting and considering my options, I decided to walk the two blocks again to the Baptist church.

This new church had recently acquired a new pastor, Duane Brown, and he gave the morning message. It was strong preaching and it caught my attention. He used God's Word to convict me, instruct me, and motivate me. With all the temptations and pressures of college life, this was helpful. With my wrestling career exploding, I was given a much-needed focus and purpose from God's perspective. I continued to attend there until I graduated.

In the spring of my junior year, Pastor Brown gave me an important statement right after I won the Big Eight Conference Championship. "Ben, you won publicly, you should thank God publicly." When I looked at him with a puzzled expression he said, "Why not give a testimony to the people at the Sunday evening service?" I agreed. I am sure I stumbled and stammered from nervousness, but I thanked God for the win and for saving me when I was in junior high.

Two weeks later I won the NCAA National Championships. When I arrived at church the next week several men greeted me with congratulations. Pastor Brown said, **"Ben, you won publicly, you should thank God publicly."** Again I stood and thanked God for the win. Pastor Brown continued to make that statement any time I won another big event.

Several of the men were strong Cyclone fans and they wanted to know more about our team. This started many conversations and I enjoyed that group.

One man in particular was Vern. He was an aggressive, confident businessman who had been a strong witness of Christ to many. Often he invited me to his home for Sunday dinner. My shyness would have preferred to go to the familiar university training table, but Vern was insistent and I went to his home several times. Decades later I still remember those visits with fondness.

Vern's younger brother was an usher and greeted me at church many times as well. Those two brothers created a perfect balance for me. The younger brother was always friendly and patient. He would talk as long or as short as I wanted. Vern was more definite and direct in teaching and challenging me. Vern is more in my memory today and I am thankful for the aggressive way he approached me. But the truth is, I may have avoided Vern completely if his quieter brother had not set me at ease and befriended me in a way that I needed.

By my senior year I was spending definite time at Campus Baptist. I attended Sunday and Wednesday services and took a couple classes at their Sunday evening Bible Institute. There were as many as a hundred college students who attended there, and the church had special activities for us. I was able to attend a few of these events.

I also got acquainted with several young men in the church who were talking of going to seminary to become pastors. Two of them were university athletes. We talked a lot about serving the Lord and they encouraged me to do the same. Those young men challenged me because they were ready to leave a solid career path to obey and serve the Lord in the various directions He was leading them. I have fond memories of those friendships.

In the end, I felt like God had prepared that group of believers just for me. It included a strong pastor, thoughtful caring older men, and young men making major career decisions and thinking through tough questions. They were all available to talk if I wanted to do so. That church was a great encouragement to me.

Above: John with college teammates and conference trophy.

Right: John's college picture - *courtesy Stout State University.*

Members of the Iowa State 1970 National Championship Team: (front row) Steve Lampe 118, Larry Munger 126, Bill Krum 134, Dan Gable (Captain) 142, Phil Parker 134, Doug Lunt 134, Doug Moses 142, Norm Wilkerson 118. (back row) Carl Adams 150, Dave Martin 158, Chuck Jean 177, Geary Murdock Hwt, Len Thompson Hwt, Ben Peterson 190, Jason Smith 177, Dave Bock 158. *(courtesy - Iowa State University)*

The 1969-70 Stout State University wrestling team won the WSUC Championship Saturday. The champs are:
Back Row: Coach Sten Pierce, John Strong, Gary Lilyquist, Tom Selvick, Leo Neville, John Peterson, Hal Dalibor-Mgr.
Front Row: Jerry Collins, Ron Gebelein, Hector Cruz, Don Heimerman, Dale Evans, Steve Henseler, Darrell Korth.
Not Pictured: Don Kirby, Larry Severson, Dan Brandl, Jerry Johnson.
(Staff Photo)

John's Wisconsin College Conference Championship team
- courtesy Stout State University.

Above: John with college teammates Hector Cruz and Dale Evans with their conference trophy.

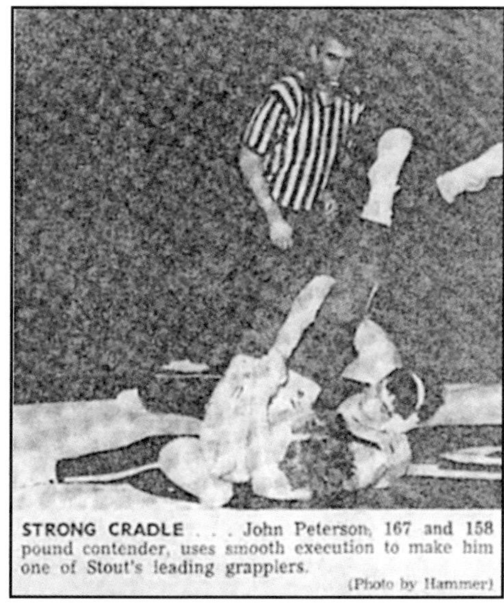

STRONG CRADLE . . . John Peterson, 167 and 158 pound contender, uses smooth execution to make him one of Stout's leading grapplers.

(Photo by Hammer)

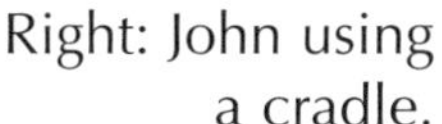

Right: John using a cradle.

Above: Carl Adams and me with Coach Nichols.

Right: Senior picture - *courtesy of Iowa State University.*

Working a cradle.

Working a crossbody ride.

Olympic Training & Munich

—28—
RESPONDING TO JOLTING EXPERIENCES

In January 1972, Dan Gable and John wrestled in the Tbilisi Tournament in the Soviet Union. While there, they were introduced to the Eastern European "sauna experience." Before wrestling, they sometimes used a sauna as part of their warm up. After all, it was mid-winter and bitter cold traveling in the Soviet Union.

The Soviet wrestlers said real men also used a "cold tub." The idea was to warm up first in the sauna, then jump into a tub of cold water for a few minutes, then get back into the sauna. The cold-water "jolt" is supposed to invigorate circulation and cleanse the body of impurities. Dan and John were told they would learn to relax and enjoy it - eventually. I wrestled in this same tournament a year later and I thought the whole sauna/cold tub experience was sheer torture. I went back three years later and the sauna/cold tub hadn't changed any.

Early in our freestyle wrestling John and I experienced extremely positive and extremely negative elements. This was similar to the Soviet sauna/cold tub.

During my senior season at Iowa State, Dan and John returned from the Tbilisi Tournament with reports of victories over the powerful Soviet wrestlers. Dan had amazed the Soviets, winning the Tbilisi Tournament by exhausting his opponents. John had a couple wins of his own. And with Iowa State winning the NCAA team championship that season and me winning a second individual NCAA championship, we seemed comfortable in our training for the upcoming 1972 Olympic trials; kind of like sweating comfortably in a nice warm sauna.

Senior Freestyle Nationals

Three short weeks after the NCAA meet in Maryland, we were all wrestling in the senior national freestyle tournament in Stillwater, Oklahoma. John and I hoped to continue our positive "sauna experience." Our freestyle skills were continually improving and our confidence was high. Our dreams were even higher. But we would soon learn the twists and turns wrestling can take at its highest level. We were about to jump out of the sauna and land in the cold tub of reality.

John and I had early victories and some compliments on our 4th place finishes. But the way each of us lost one of our matches stunned us:

- I lost 8-0 to Bill Harlow. Bill had been an NCAA champion in 1966, wrestling for Oklahoma State. He also won a silver medal at the 1970 World Championships. He is still considered among the smoothest big men in U.S. wrestling history. Bill used a high-crotch takedown continually against me. I simply was not at his level. What a jolt this one-sided loss was after winning my second NCAA championship just three weeks earlier.
- John lost 10-0 to Steve Combs. Steve had been on the Olympic team four years before, and it seemed John was not in the same league as Steve. John was repeatedly thrown to his back for back points. After all the hard training he had done in the past year, how could he still be so far behind?

After these disappointing losses, how could we ever catch up with only 1½ months before the Olympic trials? John and I were so discouraged we even talked about giving up on our wrestling dreams. To make matters more complicated, John was running out of money. Perhaps now was the time for both of us to stop wrestling, go home, and get on with life.

Changes Made and Another Change Rejected

For a few days after the senior nationals, Gable listened to our talk about not getting back into the "cold tub" again. It had been "too cold, too painful, and too jolting." Dan told John that he was being thrown on his double-leg takedowns as he was building a base to lift his opponent. He advised John to change his direction as he finished his takedowns, saying he should turn down and buckle his opponent's knees instead of predictably lifting him. For weeks after that, John drilled and drilled those double-leg takedown changes on me until the backs of my knees were sore!

As for me, I paid special attention to keeping my elbows down and bent on all my underhooks and all my collar tie-ups. The reason for doing this was to keep Bill Harlow and others like him from so easily getting under my elbows.

There was another issue I brought up with John.

"I'm just too small to wrestle at 198 pounds!" I exclaimed. So I asked him to go down to 163 so I could go down to 180.5.

But John wouldn't hear of it. He had dealt with serious weight-loss issues in college when he had tried to lose too much. Since then, he had concluded that we Petersons wrestled best when we were not cutting a lot of weight. But I still pushed him on the point, so he finally said to me, "Okay, Ben. We'll just have to wrestle for it, and we'll see who wins out on the mat."

That was the closest we ever came in our sixteen years of wrestling to an official match between us. It was just a private match in the Iowa State practice room with Doug Moses as our referee. John won the match by a single point. There is no dispute about that! So I never again mentioned going down to John's weight class. Although I occasionally complained about being too light to wrestle 198, I knew that since I was bigger than John I could compete against heavier wrestlers better than he could. This led me to develop an aggressive, scrambling style, always trying to bring a "never say die" attitude to the wrestling mat. This style enabled me to compete successfully at 198 pounds.

Still today, I am very thankful to John for vigorously disagreeing with me about whether or not he should stay at 180.5 pounds for the Olympics. Later, I realized he was definitely right. I was just trying to run away from the "jolt" that I received when I lost so decisively to Bill Harlow. **I was running away from a challenge instead of learning from it and stepping up to meet it.**

John solved his money shortage when the Iowa State coaches recommended him for a part-time job helping to maintain the field for the University's baseball team. He and my teammate, Jim

Duschen, set up the baseball bleachers and mowed the grass. Together, John and I continued to train hard with Gable in Ames. Our hopes were rebuilt, and we continued to improve.

One other dilemma facing us that spring was our sister had scheduled her wedding for the week of the Olympic trials. Since they were both near Minneapolis, we discussed making both in the same weekend. But that would not have worked. In the end, Becky and her husband, Ed, agreed to change their date by a week. In return, John and I agreed to usher.

What a contrast: Hard-nosed, conditioned wrestlers ushering at their sister's wedding! I thank Becky for changing her important day and for using us in her wedding in a special way. Our family got two great experiences instead of just one.

Olympic Trials Qualification

John was very concerned during this period of time. Finishing fourth in the nationals did not qualify him for the Olympic trials. My NCAA championship qualified me so I had no similar concerns. Gable qualified by being a World champion. I began hearing the two of them discuss how to get John in.

They determined he should go to the Iowa City regional as this was the closest qualifier. However, John and I were concerned about him beating Steve DeVries, the Iowa 177-pounder. He was tall and could be dangerous.

Since John and a few other ISU wrestlers were going, Gable thought it would be good for all of us to wrestle in it. At first I did not want to go. I was still a student and we were taking an awful lot of time for wrestling. In the end, we all went. And it was just what we needed. We all won, building solid confidence. It was helpful for John especially to move past the jolt of finishing fourth at nationals.

As we completed the wrestling and received our awards, Gable was announced as the winner at 149.5 pounds. However, he was nowhere to be found. I believe it was Doug Moses who brought news to the announcers that Dan was up in the wrestling room working out. That spoke volumes to us. He hadn't received his award from his last competition but was already training for the next one!

Olympic Trials Tournament

In May 1972, a month and a half after the senior nationals in Stillwater, John and I wrestled in the Olympic trials tournament in Anoka, Minnesota. This tournament would determine each wrestler's ranking for what was to follow in selecting the U.S. Olympic team. Anyone who won this tournament would be the top-ranked wrestler in his weight class. As such, he would only have to face one future challenger to make the team.

If, on the other hand, a wrestler finished third and still wanted to make the team, he would need to beat the wrestler ranked number two. In other words, he would have to "wrestle up the ladder." Only then would he get a tryout match with the wrestler who had won the Olympic trials tournament. That, of course, would be a tough, tough challenge for anyone hoping to make the team. It was important for us to win, or at least place high, in the tournament.

Gable was a big help to us. Before the Olympic trials, Dan had John drilling on me every day, "crunching the knees," to improve his double-leg takedown.

Sure enough, in the trials tournament John faced Combs. I missed a major part of that match. I only knew he had started well with a couple of double leg takedowns, but there was a lot of wrestling I had not seen. Quite often during the preliminary rounds, I would start my matches halfway through John's. He would start his match and I would watch from a corner where I could stay loose while waiting for my own match to begin.

When I was done with my match and congratulated by some teammates, I looked for John and asked if they knew how he had finished.

They looked at me and said, "Don't you know?!"

I turned around and saw John sitting in the corner coach's chair. He had a thoughtful look on his face, as if he was trying to let something sink in.

I went over and asked, "How'd you do?"

I watched his reply work up from his toes, through his body, and finally light up his face with a huge smile.

"I won seven to nothing!" he finally blurted out.

And he did it with a steady, controlled use of his double-leg takedown. Unlike in his earlier match against Combs just a month before, John's double-leg attack was low and disciplined with his balance maintained throughout. All the drilling that Gable had John do paid off, and he won the Olympic trials tournament.

As for Bill Harlow who had thrashed me so soundly a month before? I did not see Bill again for another 36 years. Because of his teaching and coaching obligations and because of his responsibility for his young family, Olympic training was no longer Bill's top priority. At age 29 he stopped competing and retired with a terrific record and a well-earned reputation for excellent wrestling.

Lessons Learned

Stepping up to a higher level of competition, whether in wrestling or elsewhere in life, can be stressful to any of us. Early disappointments may scare us away. Starting out as a new wrestler in high school or college, trying to make a freestyle or Greco team, or beginning a new job or a new occupation may initially bring disappointment and discouragement. If we are too shortsighted, too insecure, or lack encouragement from others, we may give up too quickly and never try again. Alternatively, we can learn from our disappointments, make necessary adjustments, and try our best again. If we do that, we may reach new heights, maybe even heights beyond our wildest expectation.

Young wrestlers should try to work through their failures and discouragements. God has given us certain abilities and opportunities. And we need to take the time, gain the knowledge, and make the adjustments to use these abilities and opportunities. We need to keep our confidence long enough and at a sufficiently high level so we can work our way through the failures and discouragements. Victory awaits those who welcome new challenges, even though those challenges may bring further disappointment.

Do not forget to help and encourage others who have suffered a loss or some other failure. Having an encouraging friend may make all the difference in the world to someone who is defeated or discouraged.

And today? I often finish a morning shower with some cool water. It's the sudden jolt that wakes me up.

—29—

A TRUE WRESTLING RIVALRY

Russ Hellickson and I were longtime wrestling rivals. We are both Wisconsin dairy farm boys who learned wrestling in the early days of the sport in our state. Russ might agree that we learned as much from our farm chores as we did from the techniques taught us by our coaches.

Russ grew up near Stoughton, a hotbed of high school wrestling in southern Wisconsin. Stoughton High School won the state team championship seven times and boasts over forty individual state champions. Russ was one of them, winning the state tournament in 1966 at 180 pounds. He attended the University of Wisconsin in Madison, and played football and wrestled. Later he dropped football to focus on wrestling. After he graduated, he was the assistant wrestling coach at Wisconsin under Coach Duane Kleven. When Coach Kleven retired, Russ became the head coach for the Badgers for five years. He left Wisconsin for Ohio State University where he coached for twenty years until his retirement in 2006.

Russ and I traveled outside Wisconsin looking for ways to improve our wrestling. Russ drove to Chicago on weekends to train with the Mayor Daley Wrestling Club led by 1960 Olympic champion Terry McCann, while I did most of my training at Iowa State.

Midlands Tournament

Russ and I first wrestled in an early round match at the 1969 Midlands Tournament. Russ was a senior at Wisconsin, and I had just made the Iowa State varsity for the first time as a sophomore. As a new member of our team, I had rising expectations. But Russ seriously out-wrestled me and won a solid victory 6-2.

A year later, I met Russ again in the Midlands, this time in the finals. I lost again, but in a much closer match 5-4. Naturally, my ISU teammates teased me about losing to a Wisconsin wrestler. They would say, "Come on, Ben, don't you know that Wisconsin wrestling isn't as tough as wrestling is in Iowa?"

When the Midlands Tournament came around over the holidays in 1971, Russ and I were ready for a wrestling match to remember. Just a few months earlier, he had won a bronze medal at the 1971 World Championships in Bulgaria. I was the defending NCAA champion at 190 pounds. After a full match in regulation time and three more overtime periods, I was declared the winner on a stalling call against Russ.

Now that our relationship is that of friends, Russ and his wife, Nancy, still like to remind me that Russ was not stalling at all in that match. Regardless, after three tries in the Midlands, I had finally beaten Russ in a college-style match. This meant I could try to finish my senior season at Iowa State undefeated.

Olympic Trials Tournament

My overtime win against Russ set the stage for the 1972 Olympic trials tournament. This tournament would set up the "ladder" for the final trials to be held in approximately two months. Both Russ and I wanted badly to be in Munich as members of the U.S. Olympic freestyle team.

After eliminating all our other opponents, Russ and I paired off against each other in the finals. Our match started, as a typical match often does, with each of us jostling for position and testing various tie-ups and takedown angles. While still in the first period, I found myself with a left-arm underhook on Russ. I might have gotten it while on my feet, although I most likely got it after attempting a double leg takedown, which Russ countered with a whizzer.

After adjusting my underhook, I tightened it, locking it around his lower chest for a bear hug. I tried to buckle Russ to the mat, but being the stronger of the two of us, he would not give in to my efforts. So we went back and forth, fiercely struggling against each other, with each of us trying to get an advantage until finally we both failed and fell to the mat.

Some memories are vivid and lasting, and this is a very vivid one. I had trained myself repeatedly over the years to scramble from one position to another and to explode whenever needed. My mind and body responded at the instant we both hit the mat. I had fallen to my backside and was sitting there with Russ on his knees immediately to my right. I had no time to lose. This could be disastrous!

Russ was also startled and out of position. I was ready to explode and was filled with the extra adrenaline from sensing myself out of position. I quickly rose while turning toward Russ and drove into him with all the force I could gather. We both crossed much of the mat and landed with Russ on his back. Under the freestyle shoulder-touch rule it was a pin, ending the match in my favor. We had so much history and many back-and-forth situations. Suddenly I was first in the Olympic trials tournament, and Russ had finished second.

About two months later, we had our final match of the 1972 Olympic trials. This match would determine who would be on the Olympic team at 198 pounds. In practice a day or two before, Russ badly injured a knee, making him a one-legged wrestler. Our finals match was mostly a formality, and I was on the U.S. Olympic team headed to Munich.

As I thought ahead about the upcoming Olympics, I wanted to do my best to top the bronze medal that Russ had won the year before in the World Championships. I also wanted to represent my home state of Wisconsin well in the Olympic Games, especially since I was responsible for eliminating one of its most talented representatives.

Post-Olympic Training

Four months after the 1972 Olympics, Wisconsin Coach Duane Kleven arranged a job for me with an architectural firm in Madison. He also invited me to train with his UW team.

At the same time I moved to Madison, Russ moved up to wrestle at 220 pounds He assured me he would stay there and not go back down to 198 as long as I stayed and trained in Wisconsin. So we trained together on a regular basis and benefited considerably. Over the years, Russ and I were teammates on two Olympic teams, three World championship teams, a Pan American team, and two World Cup teams.

Two years later, I returned to Iowa State to begin work on a

Master's degree in architecture. A man of his word, Russ went back down to 198 and beat me to make the 1975 U.S. World team. Russ had to cut a lot of weight to make 198. Meanwhile, I moved up to 220, but was much too light for that weight class, never weighing more than 208.

In 1975, Russ and I each finished fourth in the World Championships held in Minsk in the Soviet Union. On the flight home, our coaches spoke to us about switching our weight classes: Russ going back up to 220 and me going back down to 198. They thought if we switched weights, we could each win a gold medal at the 1976 Olympics in Montreal. That sounded great to us! We followed their direction and switched weight classes again. In the 1976 Montreal Olympics, we each won a silver medal.

I moved to Watertown, Wisconsin after the 1976 Olympics and Russ and I continued training together. We both retired from competitive wrestling after each of us won a spot on the 1980 Olympic team. But that's another story.

In the course of all this I met Russ's wife, Nancy. I found both Nancy and Russ to be some of the most gracious, generous, and tireless people I have ever known. They have added much to the sport of wrestling.

Today our "rivalry" includes talking to each other whenever we can, mostly about our families and, of course, wrestling. And we can stay at that for a long time! Today, Jan and I consider Russ and Nancy Hellickson to be our good friends and we wish our paths crossed more often.

—30—

AMERICA'S LEADING WRESTLING FAMILY

After we each won the 1972 Olympic trials tournament in May, John and I needed some guidance in planning our training between then and mid-July when we would start the Olympic training camp. In looking toward our training and where to do it, we surely did not know we would be looked after so well by the best wrestling family of the century, Dan Gable and his dad and mom, Mack and Kate.

When the three of us took first place at the Olympic trials tournament, Dan immediately began planning. Within an hour, he was working on ways to keep John and me around him to train until the training camp in mid-July. Dan knew that neither John nor I could train effectively in Comstock, and he knew he needed training partners. So for some reason, John and I were his pick for pre-Olympic training partners.

Olympic Training at Summer Wrestling Camps

Our first training stop with Dan took us to a wrestling camp on Lake Okoboji in northwestern Iowa for two weeks. Former Iowa State national champions Dave Martin, Tom Peckham, and Dan had organized this camp at a beautiful youth camp on a lake. Dan's understanding with us was that he would teach wrestling to the high school campers in two or three sessions every day, and after each teaching session we would wrestle with each other. Our only other real responsibility was to get a cabin full of wrestlers to fall asleep each night.

Lake Okoboji is truly a beautiful site and Gable was on cloud nine because it was wrestling all day, every day! John and I were motivated by Dan's contagious enthusiasm. And we were thankful to get three good meals a day and a good place to sleep at night. After the fast pace of our daily training, we slept so soundly we would have had little idea if a camper wandered off during the night. Dan had us up early every morning running and sprinting before breakfast.

After two weeks, we drove to Ohio for another wrestling camp where Dan was scheduled to instruct for the week. What an ideal setup these camps were! We had hard sessions by ourselves and with other top-quality wrestlers. Plus, we had young wrestlers who were learning from us and motivated by our intensity. Everyone was happy in a wrestler's world!

Interestingly, Lee Kemp was one of the young wrestlers at this camp. He later told me how motivating that camp experience was for him. He saw Gable train and wrestle, and determined to learn how to wrestle and train like Gable. Needless to say, that attitude paid off for Lee as he went on to win three NCAA titles for the University of Wisconsin and three World freestyle championships and earned a place on the 1980 Olympic freestyle team.

Our Olympic Training Facility - The Gable House

During the three weeks we were at the camps, Mack and Kate Gable were planning something special. When we finished the camp in Ohio, the plan was for John and me to join Dan and train for a full month at the Gables' home in Waterloo, Iowa. No one could have opened their home any more graciously than the Gables did and we were treated as part of their family.

Dan had many friends (mostly wrestlers), and we were neither the first nor the last to experience the Gable hospitality. If you were Dan's friend, you were treated as family. For a month in the summer of 1972, John and I were Dan's "big brothers," but only in size. We were in Dan's house, and he was the natural leader. We accepted Dan as the one in charge. Of the three of us, John is the oldest. I was the biggest but the youngest by a year and a half, and I often tried to keep up with the two of them.

Our daily training schedule started mid-morning with two hours of weight training, running, drilling, and some hard wrestling. In the late afternoon, we would commonly have another two hours of hard drilling followed by a lot of continuous round-robin wrestling.

Where did we wrestle? We drilled moves on Dan's mat in the basement of his house, and we wrestled hard in a two-car garage owned by the Cordes family. The floor sloped significantly toward the center drain, but we got accustomed to that pretty quickly.

Evening was the time Dan's imagination came alive. He would come up with unusual and fun ways to work on our cardiovascular and strength conditioning. One of his favorite tricks was for each of us to take turns doing push-ups after a run. We used a deck of cards to determine how many push-ups we would do. Unnumbered cards required fifteen push-ups. John and I would groan when we drew a high number. But Dan told us that we were actually lucky. And when he would get a low numbered card, he would be disappointed. Did you ever hear of such "logic?" "Gable Man" was always eager to work harder and longer than anyone else.

Training Harder Still

One evening before we took our showers for the second time that day, Dan told us his mom was making a special dinner. After all the work we were doing she felt we deserved an extra nice meal, so she was grilling a special cut of meat in the backyard. Mack had just come home from work, and Dan and his parents were talking by the grill. As I walked to the shower, I heard voices being raised.

By the time I finished showering, their talking included some shouting. I could tell Dan and his dad disagreed about something, which made me uncomfortable. When John finished showering, I asked him if he knew anything about the argument in the backyard.

"Not much," he said.

After listening for a few minutes, I asked John if we should leave because we had become too much of a burden. We knew Mack did not like the effect of our multiple showers every day. Water was dripping from the bathroom down into the basement. Or maybe Mack did not like the cost of all the food that three Olympic hopefuls were consuming every day.

John said, "Let's wait, Ben, and see what happens." That was good advice.

As it turned out, Mr. Gable did not think we were training hard enough! And who could blame him? When he left for work early each morning, we were still asleep. Mack was always at work and unable to see our two main workouts each day. What would you think?!

Dan came to us later that night and told us about the backyard discussion with his dad. He was unhappy to tell us his dad did not think we were doing all we could to be Olympic champions. As a result, we added pre-breakfast distance running and sprints to our training schedule. We got up early the next morning and ran hard for more than a mile and ended up at the high school track where we ran competitive sprints.

On his way to work, Mack stopped to watch us several times. This early morning running continued right up to the Olympic Games. Did we cut back our other workouts? Not at all. As our month with the Gables went on, our workouts increased and our conditioning exploded.

Dan's Level of Training

Dan often trained four times a day in sessions lasting from forty minutes to two hours. There were days he would train for eight hours. But my body just could not take that pace. As a result, Dan let me rest during one of the sessions. By the fourth week of training, I only needed one session off at mid-week. On Sunday I cut back to just an afternoon run. John kept up a bit more with Dan than I did. We were young men, and we recovered quickly. But we also saw that this type of intense training day after day could overtax the body and wear it down without giving it enough time to rest and recover. For John and me, days of rest and recovery were essential. We wanted to go to church on Sunday morning, so we did. We were learning to balance hard training with necessary recovery time. Over the next eight years of competition, this became more important.

John often talks about Gable's Saturday afternoon "marathon day." When Dan first described it to us, it hurt just to think about doing such a thing. I said, "Dan, I can't run a marathon!" The idea of marathon day for Dan was not to run twenty-six miles, but rather to run from site to site in Waterloo. The sites that he chose were just goals. For example, we did not go to the mall to shop. We went there because it was just over two miles from our previous stop and it was a good place to catch our breath. Later, John brought this idea to our Camp of Champs® programs where we go for over three hours of continuous wrestling and competitive games. Gable was the inspiration for this.

Everyday Living

Kate Gable was *chef extraordinaire* and our meals were terrific! It seemed she was in the kitchen all day long, and every meal was truly made for Olympic wrestlers. One day, I mentioned that all our workouts were bringing my weight significantly below 198. To my surprise, late that day after our evening workout, a full plate of tasty scrambled eggs and toast was waiting for me. From that time on until we left Waterloo for the Olympic training camp, Kate prepared four meals a day for me.

When I apologized to her for commenting about my weight loss and causing her to do still more work, she replied, "Ben, you can't be limited in your Olympic training. Since you are working so hard, I'll fix you the food you need to keep going every day."

Two Brief Interruptions

We had two interruptions in our training routine that summer. First, Dan had made an earlier commitment on the east coast. He preferred getting out of it, but he felt he should keep his word. The solution was to have John fly with him so they could continue their training together. It appeared I would be left behind in Iowa until news came of the death of our uncle. The Gables immediately offered me the use of Dan's car and insisted I go home to Comstock to be with my family and attend the funeral.

Three days later, we were all back in Waterloo eager to train hard for the Olympics more than ever. That short break proved to be needed. I had time with our family and came back ready to keep up with Dan and John.

Secondly, ABC Sports wanted to come and film Dan's training. They also wanted to interview him for a three-minute segment to be played during the Olympic TV coverage. Dan, of course, complained that it would interrupt our training. But in the end, he agreed to participate and I think it was helpful to all of us. The presence of ABC Sports brought a sense of reality and urgency to our preparation. At a time when our minds were filled with intense and repetitive training, the filming reminded us that the Olympics were real and would soon be upon us. Competition would be a tough challenge and all America would be watching!

Thank You to the Gables

I can't imagine how we could have been any better prepared for the 1972 Olympics than we were by spending that month at the Gable's home. Our bodies had become fully conditioned and we had reinforced each other's motivation on a daily basis. Our mental toughness was tested and strengthened every day. Our confidence in our preparation was at its peak.

Often I remember Kate Gable and her kindness to us that summer. I still wish I could thank her again personally for the best training table meals I've ever had or could ever imagine. She was a loving wife and mother, and during the summer of 1972, John and I also felt her love because we were made part of her family.

For over forty years, John and I have thought about how helpful the Gables were to us as we prepared for those Olympics. We know that we could never have done what we did in the Olympic Games without that month of training at their home. We have thanked Mack Gable many times. And after raising our own children, we realize fully what Mack and Kate Gable did for Dan, John, and me that summer.

Years later, whenever I would thank Mack for being so hard on us, he would always apologize to me. But then he would add he felt we needed a time somewhere in our training where we just "split a gut." Work explosively even while fatigued. He thought our exploding in all-out sprints while we were tired would be what we needed to win in Munich. He was right about that! I am so thankful he spoke his mind.

To close this chapter, I must again thank Dan Gable. Thank you for choosing John and me to train with you for the Munich Olympics. We are still not sure why you did it and what you saw in us, but we thank God for your generosity and for the wisdom you shared so freely with us as we trained together. You and your family were exactly what we needed to prepare to wrestle in the Olympics in Munich and later in Montreal. And we will continue to say thank you to the leading wrestling family in America.

—31—

OLYMPIC TRAINING CAMP

After a month of training with Gable at his home, we reported in mid-July to the Olympic freestyle training camp held at the University of Minnesota in Minneapolis. The purpose was to determine the ten Olympic team members and complete the training needed to compete in Munich. Much of what I remember about our training camp and some of the Olympic memories run together into a general overall impression. These are some of those memories.

Making the U.S. Olympic Team

Before we could begin the training phase, our coach, Bill Farrell from New York, needed to know who actually was on the team in each weight class. Gable, John and I had won the Olympic trials tournament in May, but we each needed to defeat one last challenger in a final tryout to make the team.

Russ Hellickson, my longtime rival, easily proved in the early matches that he was the best challenger at 198 pounds: but he badly hurt a knee while drilling in the days before his final match with me. Russ's injury left me with an empty feeling. How much satisfaction should I take in beating a one-legged wrestler? Some even suggested that others should be allowed to challenge me for the top spot. Nothing ever came of those suggestions. I beat Russ in our final tryout match, securing the 198 pound position. I was headed for Munich!

Meanwhile, John continued to build his confidence by defeating my two-year rival from Oklahoma State, Geoff Baum. After John beat Geoff in a hard-fought match, Geoff found our mother in the stands. With a stern face and a pointed finger he said, "Mrs.

Peterson, I wish you'd never had any kids!" Mom went from being startled, to laughing and talking with Geoff as he broke into a big smile. It was a compliment we have never forgotten.

Training Camp

Coach Farrell's two-a-day workouts (each two hours long) got our full attention. At least once a week, Coach brought us all together to meet as a team in a dorm room to talk. At those meetings, he convinced us all that we were the best wrestling team America had ever sent to the Olympics. He told us we would do well as a team and he made each of us believe we were fully prepared to compete at the highest level of international wrestling. He also convinced us we needed to beat every opponent we faced so decisively that an official's bad call could not take a match away from us.

Training with Gable earlier in the summer added an extra element for us. Dan, John and I, and sometimes others continued to meet to run in the morning before breakfast. We would run for a number of minutes: sprinting, darting between trees, and running on the street curbs for variety. Often in the evening after supper we would meet once again to drill, jog, or lift weights. As we continued to train together, our expectations were high. We were young and hungry to compete. We had conditioned ourselves for this long, hard, repeated training.

After our two-a-day team workouts, extra training with Gable in the early morning and again in the evening, and after Coach Farrell's regular pep talks with us as a team, John's doubts about competing at the highest level of wrestling simply faded away. His growing confidence was very helpful to me as well. When your older brother is confident, so are you!

International competition and the Olympics had once been overwhelming and indefinable and, therefore, quite intimidating. Almost without realizing it, we were learning to see the Olympics in terms of the details of an individual wrestling match. And we could wrap our brains around that!

To help keep my weight up while we worked long and hard in the summer heat, I often stopped at night for an Arby's roast beef sandwich before going to bed. Eating enough to keep my energy level up was a problem. I drank gallons of water. Although we were training at the University of Minnesota, a place famous for its snowy frigid winters, August can be hot and humid. During most of our afternoon workouts, I lost eight or more pounds.

Special Visitors and Overtraining

One afternoon, our high school wrestling coach, Jack Walsh, stopped by our Olympic training camp for a visit and brought along our younger brother Dan. It was an emotional boost to see them and for us to thank Coach once again for our great start in wrestling. During the next college season, Dan would be wrestling for North Iowa Area Junior College in Mason City, Iowa. It's amazing how their short visit could motivate us to an even higher level of Olympic preparation.

I remember that day well. After Coach Farrell's afternoon workout, we stayed and wrestled extra. Gable always had us going "one more." That day my equilibrium was not working quite right during the last fifteen minutes. I felt like someone had pulled the plug on my fuel tank. Stepping on the scale showed me why. During the afternoon workout I had lost fourteen pounds and was nine pounds underweight. I was definitely dehydrated! The photograph that Coach Walsh took of us three Peterson brothers shows our lean, drained condition. That night I had two meals, lots of water, and skipped Gable's "one more" evening workout.

Our assistant Olympic coach, Jim Peckham, told Gable, John, and me he thought we were overtraining. And, of course, he was right. As we got older, we tried hard to find the proper balance between training and recovery. But in 1972, we were still young and did what we had to do to succeed. We would often lose to older, more experienced opponents if it came to just the technique part of wrestling. So to have an edge, we needed to out-condition them. We believed at the time that all our crazy hours of hard training would pay off.

Down Wrestling

I matured in the bottom position during this time. It was a real benefit for us to learn how to wrestle on the bottom from our experienced coaches: Bill Farrell and his two assistants in the upper weights, Jim Peckham and Bill Weick. Each of them had wrestled internationally in the 1950s when, under the rules in force at that time, freestyle wrestlers were kept on the bottom for three full minutes. They knew how to turn and they knew how to counter turns.

All three of our coaches took turns wrestling with us while we were in the bottom position. And they were all three ruthless with us. It was a test we enjoyed and it left us with a renewed respect for these well-seasoned coaches. They would do whatever was needed to prepare us for Olympic-level competition, and it helped us greatly to get ready for Munich. And I know they enjoyed proving to the young generation they could still score on us.

An Odd Match

In the middle of our Olympic training, Coach Farrell would often ask us to choose a partner for a fully timed regulation match. One day, Gable and I had been drilling and sparring with each other early in practice, just as we had done throughout our time at Iowa State. So why not wrestle the timed match?

As we began, it occurred to me that I had never in those four years been in a fully timed wrestling match with Dan. Should I keep score? Would he keep score? Yes, most likely!

We began fighting for position, shooting and countering each other. Two takedowns for Dan, a takedown for me, and then a turn for me. But how would an official score my turn? Was it just one point or was it two? Did we tie, or did I win by one point?

As our practice ended that day, I thought back to Iowa State when Gable could handle me with such ease, outscoring me by dozens of points in every workout. He was now a much better wrestler than he had been back then, but had I finally caught up with him? Had I really beaten him, even just this once?

But how could I ever ask Dan about this? "Dan Gable, the wrestler, does not lose!" I respected him too much to ask him to acknowledge a loss or even a tie, even in a training match. And how could I take any real satisfaction in beating an opponent who wrestled 48.5 pounds lighter than me?! So I said nothing.

It would be twenty-five years before I had the courage and reason to ask Dan if he remembered "the match at the 1972 Olympic training camp." He nodded yes. So I asked him if he remembered who won. He simply raised his head from the autograph he was signing for a young camper and calmly said, "You."

All this put an exclamation point on the confidence that Dan Gable, Coach Farrell, and others were giving John and me. It taught me a valuable principle for making improvement in anything; put yourself in position to take your lumps from the best competitors, and then keep chasing them!

"We're Going to Munich to Win Medals, Not Be Tourists"

This short reply John gave to a question put to him by our team manager best shows what all our pre-Olympic training had done for us. John said it in Washington, D.C., where we were gathered with all the other U.S. Olympic athletes. We were there to verify passports, receive our uniforms, have our pictures taken, give some interviews, and perhaps tour a bit.

In the afternoon, we were scheduled to visit the White House and meet President Richard Nixon. But Dan and John had other plans; they wanted to get in a wrestling workout instead. So we turned our hotel room into a workout room. Those were the days before hotels had either saunas or exercise rooms. We put a towel under the door to the bathroom and turned the shower on hot to make our own steam room. We put the beds up against the walls to give us more space so we could drill moves on the carpet. It was not ideal, of course, but it worked well enough for us.

When all the other Olympians returned from visiting the White House and meeting President Nixon, our team manager, Russ Houk, came to us and asked where we were when we should have been at the White House.

John answered, "We were getting in a workout. Do you want us to go to Munich to win gold medals, or do you want us to go there as tourists?"

After hearing John's comment, Russ quietly backed out of our room and kept his thoughts to himself. A year later, Russ shared with us what he was thinking that day. He said, "Now if Gable had said that? Well, fine. But John Peterson doesn't really think he can win an Olympic medal, does he?"

John had never qualified for a high school state tournament. He had never won a national college or national freestyle championship. How could John Peterson think he was going to win an Olympic medal? But John's priorities regarding Munich were firmly set, and not even the White House or the President of the United States could divert his attention from the Olympic task at hand.

Team Chemistry

John and I respected Coach Farrell for keeping our team together during training camp and right on through the Olympics. And he did it in 1972, a time of great political and moral unrest in our country. There was the divisive Vietnam War and the accompanying anti-war movement. There was the hippie culture with its rejection of many firmly established institutions and long-standing values of our society. America was divided, and there was considerable unrest almost everywhere. In the midst of this chaos, Coach Farrell created a safe place for us to find common ground and common focus.

Rick Sanders was one of our Olympic teammates and a likable, fun-loving wrestler. In the years before 1972, he had great international success. He was on the 1968 U.S. Olympic team four years earlier in Mexico City and had won a silver medal. In the World Championships, he finished third in 1966, second in 1967, and first in 1969. Rick was an excellent wrestler with a lot of talent. He had many big wins for the U.S. in world competition. His diverse, scrambling style was also an inspiration to many of us.

What I disliked was the philosophy of the '60s that promoted immorality and a lack of personal responsibility. There was no question Rick was an outstanding wrestler, and he had the record to prove it. But the lifestyle that he openly endorsed was hurting some of our teammates. Alcohol and drug use were brought into play and hindered the success of a couple wrestlers.

One particular day, Rick brought his radio to practice to play the music of his choice. To loosen up as we began, our team ran in a big circle around the outer edge of the mats. Rick turned the volume way up until it bothered us. Several teammates asked him to turn his radio down, but he ignored their request. As we all jogged around the circle I ran by his radio, reached down, and turned it down. On his next time around, Rick turned it back up with a grin. On my next trip around, I reached down to adjust the volume again.

But in my haste, I bumped the radio and tipped it over. Rick accused me (mostly in jest) of breaking his radio.

To this day, the story is occasionally told that Rick and I were enemies and that I broke his radio. The truth is, I greatly respected Rick as a wrestler and teammate. I did, however, disagree with some of his actions.

You may find yourself in similar situations with teammates whose lifestyles you disagree with, but who can be valuable teammates as you seek to improve together. Who knows what effect our actions will have on others? We need to choose our actions wisely!

Team Goals

A theme that united our team was our desire to finish ahead of the Soviet Union and the other Eastern Communist Bloc countries where wrestling was (and remains) strong. Countries in Eastern Europe were usually our chief rivals. At the time, the Cold War divided the world into two major "blocs," and this division played itself out in international sports, particularly wrestling. Coach Farrell was not afraid to motivate and unite us on the theme of patriotism.

As you can imagine, patriotism at its best was present. As members of the U.S. Olympic team, we were motivated beyond ourselves. Our faith in God and our desire to proudly represent the U.S. motivated John and me to train hard and compete at a level we had never known before.

—32—

FIRST OLYMPIC IMPRESSIONS

The final days before competition in Munich were filled with intensity and sporadic relaxation. Training, formal team activities, friendships, and foreign travel demanded our attention.

Preparing To Compete

For many decades, the U.S. Olympic Committee has given special attention to our Olympic athletes. By 1972, the Olympic Committee knew just how to outfit our team. Along with over 600 athletes and coaches, we spent three days in Washington D.C. being outfitted by Sears, Roebuck & Co. They were the supplier and they did a great job. We were given multiple sets of warm-ups, workout gear, parade uniforms, and a suit to help us look our best whatever the occasion. Each team member also received a camera from Kodak and various other items. We were ready both to compete and to do a little sightseeing on the side.

As Olympic athletes, we were so well equipped that as we left the U.S. we needed few, if any, of our own personal items. In fact, the Olympic officials instructed us to mail most of our personal belongings home before leaving the States.

When we arrived in Munich by charter flight, our coaches first gave us some time to sleep and settle into our tenth-floor apartments in the newly constructed Olympic Village. The Village was an architectural designer's dream. All the Olympic buildings, including the Village, were either brand new or newly remodeled to take on the Olympic theme. My architectural interest in all this building construction and renovation would have to wait: Coach Farrell was calling us to practice.

Under the established Olympic schedule, freestyle competition was set for the first five days of the Games. Our team arrived ten days early to get acclimated to our new surroundings. Each day we took a bus to the training building for our practices. In the midst of thousands of athletes and coaches, our team members found their way to the bus for a ride to our workout site. Focused intensity is a strong memory of the Munich Olympics.

Teammates

Sergio Gonzalez (105#) was a bubbly, talkative man until he cut the last few pounds to make weight.

Jimmy Carr (114.5#) was the same, but the coaches were surrounding him to help him deal with so many new experiences and situations. He was only seventeen and by far the youngest. Chris Taylor and I were next at twenty-two.

Rick Sanders (125#) was ribbing with the coaches and any who would join him. His light-hearted confidence was refreshing for many of us.

Gene Davis (136#) was sober and serious. He had been in many levels of wrestling for years, but this was the Olympics.

Dan Gable (149#) was on a mission. His only thought and conversation was focused on winning.

Wayne Wells (163#) had a quiet confidence and deep commitment to win. This was not much different than how he appeared for over a month.

John (185#) soaked in the whole setting and continued to gain confidence.

(198#) I was nervous and excited all at once.

Henk Shenk (220#) was quiet most of the time. I don't recall much conversation with Henk, but I am pretty sure he was nervous along with the rest of us.

Chris Taylor (unlimited heavyweight) was lighthearted most of the time. But he, like me, was unproven and looking forward to the competition. I think he wanted to get started so he could prove to people he was a gifted, disciplined athlete and not merely a big man.

There was a simple excitement about us being ready and anxious to prove ourselves. This was my first time traveling outside the United States. I heard many strange languages, and I saw many people who were in some ways diverse, and yet in other ways so much like us. The strangeness of everything worked in ways to my advantage. Being among the younger wrestlers on our freestyle team, I let the others try to communicate for me.

The communicating I saw was fascinating! My teammates used sign language, repetition, some guessing, and a lot of laughter to communicate with people from other cultures and languages.

Our coaches emphasized the need to focus first on the Olympic task at hand, which was to wrestle at our very best. So I avoided tourism and peaked my training one more time. Gable, John, and I worked hard right up to opening day. Jim Peckham told me later that he thought we were overworking on the last few days before competition and he may have been right. But since I was just twenty-two, my time for recovering from our hard training was noticeably shorter than it would be for some of the older men.

The Olympic Village provided brief moments of diversion. For example, all day and much of the night, the Olympic dining hall had the best food of every kind imaginable! It served hard-working athletes from every culture around the world, and it was definitely prepared to do so. It was hard not to overeat!

Dan Gable received respect from foreign athletes wherever he went. Our entire American freestyle team may have been known to many Americans, but at the Olympics it was Dan who others knew as our superstar. He attracted the attention of the press and would be surrounded and interviewed more often than he thought best for his training. As always, though, he took the time to answer questions even as he worked hard on his final wrestling preparations.

Chris Taylor, our 400+ pound heavyweight, also brought out the cameras. He was by far the biggest athlete at these Olympic Games and everyone around him was in awe. They wondered if he could move and adjust on the wrestling mat. Chris was a jovial, fun-loving, energetic man who loved being the comedian on our team and who loved joking around with the fans. The attention was fine for a while, but it did begin to tire him out.

Chris's size had become almost ordinary to me. I had spent eighteen months training with him, and I had learned how to get him tired, how to take him down, and how to turn him for a pin. Chris was a delightful teammate at Iowa State and on the Olympic team, and he had become a good friend.

A day or two before competition began, Chris and I were kidding around in our Village apartment. I teased him about his size as I punched him gently in the stomach. He warned me, "Don't do that, Ben." He tightened up his stomach muscles, and I could feel them like bands of steel allowing him to move all that weight around so smoothly. I was feeling too playful, and I kept punching him gently from the side. As I got to his shoulder, he repeated again, "Ben, don't do that!"

The next thing I knew, Chris took a little hop, leaned slightly to his left, and put a right-foot karate kick up at my nose. I was startled and amazed as I blinked, expecting his foot to land on my face. As my eyes opened, his foot was back down bouncing on the floor again. With a stern grin, Chris said again, "Ben! Don't do that!" I apologized to him and assured him I would never punch him in the stomach like that again, even in jest.

I was amazed by what I had just seen. If Chris had not been such a controlled and disciplined athlete, he may have seriously hurt me with his karate kick. Instead, his agility and control made all this just child's play to him. I have never done a karate kick like that in my life! An occurrence like this can deepen and even help define a friendship. Using his terrific body control, Chris took my untimely kidding and deflected it with a stern but friendly grin and a firm, "Don't do that, Ben." We respected each other even more after that incident.

Cold War

In 1972, the Cold War between the United States and the Soviet Union affected the Olympics. As athletes representing the U.S. we knew we would compete against the Soviet Union and its Eastern European allies. We had heard stories about these Soviet-bloc teams working together: even deliberately losing a match to aid each other in fixing the results in World and Olympic competition. Needless to say, this deliberate manipulation could lead to tension among the athletes.

At times however, there were smiles and greetings across the Cold War divide. For example, John played a friendly game of chess with an athlete from the Soviet Union. They moved life-size chess pieces on a large chess board built into the ground in the Village courtyard. As they played, they kidded each other about the World Chess Championship that Bobby Fischer (the reigning champion from America) had just won earlier that year by beating the defending champion, Boris Spassky of the Soviet Union.

The press noted that John and the Soviet athlete played chess together in the Olympic courtyard. It was unique enough to be mentioned by the reporters and it made for a good story about an American athlete and a Soviet athlete brought together by sports. Both athletes were in Munich doing their best to defeat their Olympic opponents. For a few minutes in the middle of their preparations it was great for them to simply play a friendly universal game.

The Press

Several journalists arranged for interviews with John and me. We had spoken together earlier of our desire to talk to others about our faith in Jesus Christ. But we were both shy and reserved about it, wondering how it could be done appropriately.

But God dealt with our nervousness. When reporters interviewed us, they would often quote from an earlier article already published in a New York newspaper and ask, "What's this all about, that you are going to Munich to win gold medals for America and to tell others about God?" With that introductory comment and its follow-up questions, it was easy for us to tell reporters about trusting Jesus Christ as our Savior in junior high. Our faith was written about in several major U.S. newspapers. After the Olympics were over, Mom received copies of many of these articles from people who had been encouraged by our testimony.

Opening Ceremony

The Opening Ceremony is more for the fans than it is for the athletes. This is particularly true for those competing the day after the ceremony. Gable did not want to go, John wanted to rest, and I was divided in my thoughts. In the end, we decided to go. It was long, mostly in other languages, and hard to see.

John's memory is much the same, but he also remembers sitting on the ground and talking during the ceremony with J Robinson and Wayne Baughman, members of our Greco-Roman team. They offered interesting and entertaining conversation that was memorable for us. Our intense training schedule and our continual focus on winning needed to be mixed with some relaxation and something fun as well.

We were a group of wrestlers with entirely different backgrounds, personalities, and ages. We had no dull moments leading up to our competition! We had fun together and the passion and intensity that wrestling demands created a tight-knit group ready to face the competition together with enthusiasm. That is what was so terrific about our 1972 Olympic team.

—33—
A DIFFICULT OLYMPIC WEIGH-IN AND A GOOD DRAW

What could possibly be memorable about a weigh-in at the Olympic Games? By the time I reached Munich I had weighed in hundreds of times. So what was so noteworthy about another weigh-in, even an Olympic weigh-in?

It was the day after the Opening Ceremony and my thoughts were on breakfast. But first I needed to show that I had made weight. When I weighed myself that morning, I was surprised to learn that I was a pound over my 198 pound limit. After worrying for months about being too light, I now needed to run in order to make weight. Although I knew it would be no problem to get down in time, it meant I would miss the first weigh-in cycle and the first shuttle to breakfast! This annoyed me greatly.

I ran for fifteen minutes and lost the pound, lecturing myself the whole time for not monitoring my weight more carefully. Gable and John also commented on the need for urgency.

Soon I would learn an important lesson about what life was like for our 105-pounder, Sergio Gonzales. Sergio was just over half my size and only one-fourth the size of Chris Taylor. For Sergio to make weight, he had to struggle mightily to get rid of every extra ounce.

I saw him, struggling and looking exhausted, get on the scale again with just minutes left on the clock. The balance still showed Sergio had not made weight. The Communist-bloc official monitoring the scale saw maybe he could end any challenge on the mat from Sergio and immediately declared weigh-ins were now over.

Our coaches - Farrell, Peckham, and Weick - responded instantly! Looking at the clock, they saw a couple more minutes remained where Sergio could properly weigh in. While one of our coaches confronted the official at the scale with the truth about the time, a second coach called for our medical kit. I ran to help him find it while asking, "Coach, why do you want the med kit?"

He yelled after me, "Just get it, Ben! Just get it!" When I handed him the med kit, he grabbed the scissors out of it and ran over to Sergio. Why?

It was 1972 and long hair was "in." And this was Sergio's choice in hairstyle. While he was still standing on the scale, Coach started cutting big chunks of hair off the back of Sergio's head. The weight-monitoring official saw what was happening and concluded that Sergio had, indeed, now made weight. Just that quickly, the weigh-in was over. Sergio had made his weight, and we were on our way to breakfast. That was an adventure for me that morning, but a close call for Sergio.

At the time, I was rather disappointed with the extended wait for breakfast and with the shortened time for rest before my first match. Later, I appreciated the value of fully understanding that even weigh-ins could be surprising at the Olympics. What our coaches had often warned us about in competing during the Cold War had come to life for me that day. Cut-throat elimination, manipulation, and more were now reality and not just idle talk.

Honestly, I did not fully grasp the seriousness of all this when we were told about it in our training camp. Did we really need to watch our backs all the time? Certainly the officials and opposing coaches would know and acknowledge the truth. But we were repeatedly reminded to do our best whenever we could to avoid being "close" in a match for fear that an official might try to make a "quick call" and actually get away with it. We were told to "be as far from close as possible" and were told to "win big so there is no question."

After witnessing Sergio's weigh-in, I saw on the very first day that our coaches were not chasing conspiracy theories and they were ready to jump instantly to our aid whenever necessary. They were watching carefully at all times, and on the very first day of the Olympics their diligence paid off!

John's Good Draw

A wrestler's draw is extremely important in the Games because there is no seeding based on a wrestler's past success or failure.

There is no criteria to determine who wrestles who first. You pray a lot asking God for a good draw.

It had only been a year since the World Championships in Bulgaria where John had lost his first two matches and he wondered who from that tournament had qualified for the Olympics. Scanning his own bracket and the rosters of the other countries, he saw that both of the men who had beaten him had made their respective teams and were at the Olympics. John began to wonder if he would have to face either of them right away. He fretted about this until the draw was announced and pairings were listed. John was pleased at our first weigh-in to learn he had drawn the wrestler from Great Britain, which was not a wrestling super power. He thinks he benefitted greatly by getting some easier matches at the start of his Olympic competition.

I have often said our path through life has God's fingerprints all over it. John's good draw in the early round was another confirmation of this fact. Do we believe God used some hocus-pocus in drawing a name out of a hat? Hardly. Do we understand He controls the daily details of our lives? Yes.

—34—
OUR FIRST OLYMPIC MATCHES

The first match in any big tournament often sets the tone for the rest of the meet. This is true whether it's elementary school level, high school, college, or beyond. And it is equally so in the Olympic Games.

John's First Match

John began his first-round match with enthusiasm and confidence. This came from his thorough preparation and from what he saw his teammates already doing.

He entered his first match against Richard Barraclough of Great Britain, confident that his chances of winning were good. And early in the second period, John turned Barraclough with a half nelson. Just like that, John had won his first Olympic match by a pin!

Pavel of Poland

My first match was against Pavel Kurczewski of Poland. He was shorter than me, stocky and strong. After sparring a bit, I decided to directly attack his legs. Of course, it is usually best not to charge directly into a tree trunk! Before long, he had me in a front headlock. His stocky body was made for stability, and he was trained to clamp and throw his opponents. I should not have given him any opportunity to tie up my head, but I did.

During the previous four years, whenever I had gotten my head down on a takedown attempt in the Iowa State practice room, the Cyclone wrestlers had punished me repeatedly with strong front headlocks. Dan Gable, Chuck Jean, Jason Smith, Dave Martin, Tom Peckham, Jim Duschen, Rich Binek, and many others had turned me for back points and often pinned me using a front headlock. John also used front headlocks on me. As a result, I learned to avoid the front headlock.

However, I also learned to be determined whenever I was caught in one, and to hold my ground. Now, in my first Olympic match, I was caught in a front headlock by an experienced wrestler. Pavel was trained in upper-body Greco-Roman wrestling, and he knew front headlocks better than many other elite wrestlers.

I tried to retreat and get back on my feet. Pavel would have none of it. He tightened his lock on my head and arm, trying to score his own points. I worked to stay mobile and off my knees with my free hand on the mat. I knew significant weight on my free hand could limit his control. I tried to break his headlock and free my trapped arm, but he just tightened the headlock even more. I was in serious trouble!

Unlike what American high school and college rules emphasize, controlling me was not Pavel's goal in this freestyle match. Rather, what he wanted to do was earn back points by turning my back to a 90-degree-or-less angle with the mat. After several seconds had passed, and after he had made some adjustments and re-tightened his lock, I could sense he was going to try to turn me. I was working way too hard this early in the match and I knew I would pay dearly for it later. But I also knew I could NOT afford to let him turn me for back points.

Pavel was two months younger than me and it was like two young rams with their horns locked for the fight. He had the advantage, but I had the clarity of knowing I could not afford to be turned so early in the match. I spread out my long legs and arms, and held my ground. Whether you call it determination, stubbornness, or just plain bullheadedness, I knew that I must stand my ground.

Pavel decided it was time to turn me. I said to myself, "NO WAY!"

I am still thankful for making that decision, which might sound somewhat out of place in a sport that often relies on automatic reactions and reflexes created from years of training. But I had time to decide, and I stood my ground until he lost his grip and slipped under me. The next thing I knew he was scrambling off his back. To work his way out, he tried to flurry. I turned him to his back a second time, earning five points in a matter of seconds.

The rest of the match was a blur. We both spent a lot of energy in an extended standoff. My early points were enough to hold off his frantic attempts to score at the end of the match. I walked off the mat exhausted, but I had won on points 7-4.

Coaches Farrell and Peckham quizzed me vigorously about being so tired at the end of this first match. My only response was that I was too nervous at the beginning and had tired myself in an effort to withstand Pavel's early attempts to turn me with the front headlock.

If I had given in to him on the front headlock, he could have easily ended the match with a pin and likely given me a short Olympic career. My confidence at the time would have been totally different than it was after I won this first match. With a first-round loss, I would have been wondering about myself as an Olympic wrestler. Instead, although I was sobered by the intensity of the competition, I also knew firsthand that I could deal with it. I assured my coaches that I would be more careful to avoid such energy-draining situations in future matches.

Looking back, the standoff against Pavel Kurczewski of Poland set a pattern for me to follow for the rest of the '72 Olympic matches and also for eight more years of international wrestling.

I was more careful to avoid opening myself to an opponent. I worked hard to avoid the "locking of horns," while also knowing that I would, and could, withstand it if necessary. You do not get behind on the scoreboard to a wrestler like Pavel and hope to come back. Later, he showed me this was true by beating me twice in the next two years. I would face him again in the 1976 Olympics in Montreal in another tough battle before finally outscoring him again. Whenever I got behind him in points, it was always difficult to score.

My advice to young wrestlers is to be cautious about opening yourself up too much to your opponent, especially early in a match. But if you do get locked up in a bad wrestling position, it may become a "do or die" situation for you earlier than you would like. You must be aggressive and push the action, but always be ready to stand your ground. No one likes to scramble on the mat more than I do, but you'll pay dearly if you expose yourself to a tight, dangerous hold.

If you do get caught, stand your ground to the very end. Understand that you will be significantly fatigued after withstanding a situation where you have given the other wrestler the advantage. Yet, if you can withstand and survive without giving up points, you may have two other advantages. The other wrestler will likely be fatigued from attempting to take advantage of the position. And, just as important, he will have been unable to capitalize on his clear advantage. This realization can be very discouraging and distracting to your opponent. No matter what, decide to resist!

—35—
DAYS 2 AND 3 CLIMBING HIGHER

Winning our first Olympic matches was enormous for John and me. In fact, winning your first match anytime is a big confidence booster. There is often uncertainty and a lot of nervousness before a tournament, so it was good to be able to beat anyone who made it to the Olympics.

John has always felt very fortunate, since others had their hardest opponent the first round. Sergio Gonzales started out against the World champion and tied him. Chris Taylor wrestled 2-time Olympic champion and 7-time World champion, Alexander Medved, and lost 3-2 in the first round. Even with their tough draws, our teammates were wrestling well.

Rick Sanders used his experience to out-slick his opponents. He had been the USA's first World freestyle champion three years earlier and we knew Rick had the potential to do well in Munich.

At 163, Wayne Wells was wrestling hard with the sharp pain of a rib injury. Gable was relentlessly pursuing excellence, giving up no points to anyone. John got to see me doing well, and I am sure felt a little extra challenge to make sure he did not let his younger brother outdo him.

These matches set the stage and the mood for our intensity. I really wanted Chris to win, and it was so close. But Medved operated like a seasoned veteran. He knew how to stall and control the pace yet look good. And just when it looked like he would be called for stalling, he chose a simple leg-trip and scored the one point he needed. I learned a lot from watching my teammates that first day.

John and I knew we would soon face the tougher people in our weights so we were thankful to start as we did. We slept with grateful hearts that first night and excitement for what was yet to come.

Day 2

The next day, John wrestled Peter Neumair of West Germany. He found Peter strong and hard to penetrate with his shots. In the third period John sensed Peter beginning to tire. Keeping up the hard attacks, John scored more than once and increased his lead to a strong win. Although we do not have videos or films of this match, we both recall strong confidence being built and confirmed. John was now 2-0 in Olympic competition. This was a nice reversal from his previous summer's record of 0-2 in the World Championships.

My second match was with Raul Garcia of Mexico. At the end of the first period, I led 5-0. During this match the officials cautioned both of us for stalling. I lost a point for stalling while scoring a lot of points. Coach Farrell's warning was true. It was good to have that call. I knew they expected continual action and attempts to score. I quickly got a bear hug to a takedown and back whipped him for two back points. After getting a solid lead, it became possible to pin him. The score was 13-1 when I pinned him at 8:09. John and I were finding our conditioning to be a key element in our ability to wear down an opponent and score big at the end. I would find that pin essential later on.

Day 3

John Faces Poland

A particularly important match for John was his third round match against Jan Wypiorczyk of Poland. A year earlier at the World Championships, Wypiorczyk had beaten John 4-2. In this Olympic match, Jan and John exchanged points in the first two periods and were tied 3-3 after five minutes of wrestling. At one point, the Pole countered John's 2-on-1 with a quick ankle block with his own foot. (Later I would learn this move well enough so John could practice countering it.) They were still tied going into the third period. Wypiorczyk was of stocky build and shorter than John, and when John got the underhooks to a bear hug and hoisted him in the air it was impressive! The result was a takedown. Then he did his double for another takedown. With a 5-3 lead, John sensed Jan was fatiguing and he pressed the action. He controlled Wypiorczyk with a 2-on-1 to a double leg, and finally "double trouble," pinning him in 6:35. John's look of satisfaction and new confidence was obvious as the referee raised his hand.

Twelve months of relentless training had completely turned the results around. John had a long ways to go yet, but he reversed his previous loss with a pin. He has repeatedly stated, "I felt cheated when Wypiorczyk gave up at the end and let me pin him." John hated that, and did not believe wrestlers would just quit in the Olympics. But indeed, that is what happened. John felt good and was grinning a lot with his three wins, which included two pins. It was a long ways from two and out as he had done in the previous World Championships.

With his win over Wypiorczyk in round three, John's enthusiasm and confidence rose to new heights. John has emphasized to me that he had learned the importance of simply wrestling to the best of his ability while leaving the results entirely in God's hands. John learned to do this rather than putting a lot of pressure on himself to win as he had often done in high school and college. This simple change of mindset made a big difference in his performance and is what allowed him to capitalize on all the extra exposure to elite training partners and coaches.

I Face the Soviet

The third day was a significant test for me. Gennadi Strakhov of the Soviet Union had been World champion two years before, and I knew I had my hands full. After all the talk all year about the Soviets, I was now facing off with one of their successful ones.

Right from the beginning of the match, we respected each other's skill and threat for scoring. By the end of the first period the referees were warning both of us for passivity. Then in the second period they penalized each of us for a point. My double leg takedown attempts were not getting very deep and Strakhov countered them so easily that the official was accusing me of not trying hard enough. But I was not going to be careless and expose myself foolishly and give him easy points. Too many times he got double underhooks and I had to fight my way to inside control and get my own underhooks. I had pummeled considerably at training camp and now realized I would need it for the full nine minutes.

Then Strakhov reached for an inside single. He got my left leg high enough to take my foot off the mat. It was the closest thing to risky he had done the whole match and I was going to make him pay for it. Adrenaline was high and my focus was at its peak. He was out of position and we both knew it. It's never a good time to shoot when you're out of position. Either he would score or I would. Securing his right arm with my left arm "whizzer" and stuffing his head down with my right hand, I trapped his head under my chest and hip weight. Then crowding my right side closer to him, I blocked the back of his right knee with my left foot and his left knee with my right hand. Releasing the pressure on his head, it popped up and he fell backwards. Strakhov seemed surprised and unsure of how to deal with that position. He was stocky and shorter than me and my leverage had worked to my advantage. The officials awarded only one point for control/takedown. The move was actually taught to me as a fun little "clinic" move, but it worked great that day!

Let me pause here to say all wrestlers experience what we call "aha" moments, and this was one of those for me. We don't always remember the details of every match, but as I watch the video today of this one with Strakhov, it reinforces what I have rehearsed in my memory all these years. I must admit, I enjoy watching this match! But back to the action...

I was now leading 2-1. He just kept coming forward looking to tie up and push me, hoping I would get out of position and expose myself. His pressure was relentless and I fought back the same way. Then I was called for stalling again at 5:42 which tied the score at 2 each.

I continued to shoot singles and doubles, getting to his legs only occasionally as he sprawled hard. At one point he countered a double with a front headlock. I got off my knees and drove him out of bounds. No more front headlocks on me!

At 8:42 he got me in a double underhook. He shrugged his shoulders and got to the side with a bear hug. (It was similar to what Medved had used to score on Chris Taylor in the final minute of their match.) I immediately tightened my whizzer on his arm, putting pressure on his shoulder. Then using my long leverage, I faced him and arched my back to break his lock around my chest. This recent action was the most aggressive effort he made to score. We pummeled for inside position to finish the nine minutes.

In the end it was still 2-2, but I had tied the Soviet World champion! That was an enormous encouragement to me. I knew then I was at the level of the best in the world. But how could I get the gold without defeating him? Knowing the round robin system they used gave me the answer. I must beat others more soundly than he did. There were still ten men in our weight class; we were only half done wrestling.

In the stands Mom, Dad, Phil and his fiancée Rita, were getting smiles on their faces. They had not traveled halfway around the world to watch John and me be eliminated, and we were now in solid positions to work for medals. They congratulated us and hurried to their bus for the hour-long ride to the village where they had rented rooms in homes like the rest of the wrestling families.

Looking at the video of the Strakhov match, I see a style of wrestling used by the Soviets that was very pushy and sought to keep forward pressure, yet with a stance that was ready to defend against attacks. He literally took only one shot at my legs. It seems he was waiting for me to break mentally and leave good position so he could get the advantage to score. That backfired on him and I scored when he made the one fatal attempt at my legs. We both needed more risk-taking to actually score on each other.

Maybe he was hoping for the official to penalize me again to disqualify me. He showed little urgency in all of this. I am glad I did not overexpose myself against him.

All I can say is I was well prepared by the endless hours of training at Iowa State, with Gable, and with John. Plus my three Olympic coaches, Farrell, Weick, and Peckham, had drilled pummeling, position, and toughness into me.

As the referee raised both of our hands, we looked exhausted and both looked down at the mat. As we were turned to face the opposite side of the arena, I looked up. Strakhov never looked up.

In the end it was a mental victory for me. He was the seasoned World champion and I had just tied him and scored the only offensive point.

—36—
DAY 4
SETTING THE STAGE FOR THE FINALS

John Faces the World Champion

This would be a big day for us. We would each wrestle two matches. In the morning John faced Levan Tediashvili of the Soviet Union. Levan is from Georgia between the Black Sea and the Caspian Sea where many of the top Soviet wrestlers came from. The previous January, John had lost to Tediashvili in the Tbilisi Tournament and again at a dual meet in the north Caucasus Mountains. At a dual in Minnesota, Levan won 4-2 in a close match. He had also won the World Championships the summer before.

Could John make it different this time? John took Levan down with more than one double leg. Twice John had Levan in a bear hug but lost it and got scored on. (Greco-Roman Olympian Jim Gruenwald later told John that if he had known more Greco he might have thrown Levan.) Nine minutes later the score was 13-4 in Levan's favor. I believe John realized his early wins were the real deal, but that the best in the world are still an entirely different level.

Two times John was deep on his single and double leg takedown attack when the referee stopped the match to call Levan for locking on John's throat and then for stalling. What would have happened if those takedown attacks had not been stopped? But John was not ready to deal with the situations where Levan scored big. John pushed the pace hard to the end, but in too many tough positions Levan took the upper hand and prevented any comeback attempts from John.

John never beat Tediashvili, often regarded as one of the best wrestlers ever from any country. Over the years, however, John and

Levan have become friends. Since the 1972 Olympics, John has seen Levan several times at international wrestling tournaments and visited Levan in his home. Levan has also visited John in his home in Comstock, proving that wrestling rivals can become friends even across the oceans.

I Meet the Iranian

For my first match of the fourth day, I faced Reza Khorrami of Iran. We did a lot of hard sparring and pummeling. Reza was short and stocky and knew how to position himself on his feet. When I shot my doubles, he lowered his hips and met my attack.

Three or more times I thought I might score, but he made it out of bounds. Even though I got in deep, he found a way to escape my scorings.

He began shooting singles and I stuffed his head down each time. At the end of the first period the score was 1-1. Each of us had found a way to score on one control.

In the middle of the third period, he shot a head outside single. Sprawling and trapping his shoulder down, I worked a turn that lifted his hips over his head and exposed his back for two points. He settled out and looked surprised at the turn. It was the kind of tilt I would use multiple times over the next few years.

He tried one more single, but I stuffed his head again. It appeared the single was his key and maybe only attack. With the partial videos we have, it appears I won 4-1. Without that video, I have very little memory of that match.

After nine minutes of hard fought wrestling I had won by points. The Iranians are tough competitors. They know the game, and it is very hard to get them out of position. But I was learning to be relentless on attacks using doubles and singles and countering my opponent's attacks. In the end I "shaped him," and he just could not go at my pace for nine minutes.

There was talk that the Iranian team had been greatly distracted in their training by the Iranian Civil War that was currently raging between the Shah and the radical Muslim Ayatollah leader. We felt blessed and fortunate to be Americans with a mostly-stable society. It's a lot easier to train for a sport when your country's daily life does not involve conflict.

Round 5 - the Evening of Day 4

John completed the day against the Romanian. From the beginning, Vasile Iorga kept a low stance with good pressure. John countered Iorga's singles and pressed for his own doubles. One result of countering multiple singles is you get caught in a front headlock occasionally. Twice this happened with John and he had to keep a strong position until Vasile backed off.

With John leading 3-2 after two periods, he continued to press for doubles and scored twice more to win 5-2. As we watch the brief part of the match we have on film, John is continuing to push to score at a pace the Romanian could not match. As a result, Iorga found himself too consumed with countering to set up his own good takedown attempt.

That solid win put John in strong position for a silver medal. He would now face the East German on the final day of competition.

Barbaro Morgan of Cuba was my next task. He was tall, flexible, and strong. Wrestling tall men was not my favorite thing to do. They seemed clumsy to me, and I suppose other people felt that way about me. I liked being the tallest.

Getting an early single leg takedown, Barbaro took a one-point lead. He continued to look for a single as I sought to get my own shots on him. He escaped a couple by getting out of bounds. I kept trying to control his head when he shot.

Attempting a single, he moved up to a bear hug which surprised and scared me. He started to bring me to my back. Immediately I gave him control and back points but I leveled out to my belly. Freestyle turns really make a wrestler conscious of shoulder control. I quickly gave up control to keep from falling to my back for a possible fall. The first period ended 3-0 in his favor.

We were working at a solid pace and I was concerned but not panicked. I sensed Morgan was getting tired. If your condition is good and you know you can keep going faster and harder than your opponent, there is no need to fear or panic when behind by three. You can match those points in a later period. However, you cannot wait to pressure. You must do that all along.

I got in deep on a couple doubles in the second period. He countered using a whizzer and the edge of the mat. That happened more than once. Then he shot again with his head down so I could stuff it under my hip and a real battle ensued. This was the position for me to take command! I was stopping his strength, the single attack, and turning it into my scoring position.

First, you must stop your opponent's momentum; I did that. Then you must make him vulnerable. So I swung my hips and legs back and took him to the mat. Often an opponent will let go at this point and bail out: Morgan chose to keep the leg and went to his knees. I continued to sprawl and circle, stretching his arms, shoulders, and body.

Then he let go. I quickly moved behind and went for the arm-bar on his right side. Collecting it up tight to my hip, I began driving with authority. There is no time to delay in freestyle wrestling when on top. You have 10-15 seconds to accomplish something or you will be put back on your feet. In college, we used arm-bars with patience and position. But now, I drove it like a galloping horse, punching with my hip as we went.

The Cuban tried to squeeze his arms in. He really needed to turn hard away from me but as he rolled over, he delayed on his shoulders. That was all I needed. Two of the three referees called for a pin. As the ref blew his whistle, we both looked up with surprise at how fast it was called. It was quick, and it gave me another pin. This was huge.

My coaches and teammates were elated with my win. I remember the coaches being busy with other wrestlers so they did not immediately meet with me to assess my medal situation. I knew, however, that I was now a medal contender. On the way back to the Olympic Village, the seasoned wrestlers like Wayne Wells and Rick Sanders warned me of my status with three Communist bloc wrestlers and me still alive for the next day. More than once that evening I regretted tying the Soviet. But out of five Olympic matches I now had two wins by points, two pins, and a tie!

In addition to John and me, four other U.S. wrestlers were still alive at the end of our fourth day: Rick Sanders, Dan Gable, Wayne Wells, and Chris Taylor. All of us were in position to earn a medal. We went back to the Olympic Village with strong hopes for the next day. Could we win multiple gold medals? Rick Sanders at 125, John at 180.5 and Chris Taylor at heavyweight each had one loss, but were in strong positions for silver medals. Dan Gable at 149 and Wayne Wells at 163 were undefeated after five rounds. And I had the one tie, but still had the chance to win gold. We all were confident of getting a medal. Tomorrow would be a big day!

—37—
DAY 5
WHAT MEDALS WILL WE EARN?

Sometimes a wrestler can think too much. That is what I did the night before the fifth and last day of competition. The reality of my situation set in as I was getting ready for bed. By the next morning I was very distraught.

Three Communist wrestlers and one free world American in the same round-robin is trouble. After hearing all the things to watch for with matches being "thrown" to help other Communist wrestlers, I was very unsure of my chance at any medal, much less a gold one. I voiced disgust with my tie two days earlier and that my chance for any medal could be taken away. Coach Farrell heard my statements. He had also been awake thinking how each wrestler was positioned. He knew about my status and he knew how to watch and avoid being cheated.

The next thing I knew, Coach Weick was at my side telling me how I could still win the gold. I thanked him for being positive, but I told him I did not like the setting I was in. So he brought me to the large bracket for my weight class. Step by step he walked through what would happen if I lost, if I won, and if I pinned the Bulgarian. He assured me all the coaches believed I could pin him. He said little about the fact that the Bulgarian had won the World Championships the previous year.

While urging me to stay positive, Coach Weick showed me excitement about the hopes he, Coach Farrell and Jim Peckham had for me. I weighed in and got my breakfast with an entirely new mindset. Hope was still alive, but I needed to work extremely hard for another pin.

I also recall Rick Sanders easily beating his opponent that morning. He was miles ahead of even his final round opponents.

Gable won easily as well. Having your teammates win can build your confidence, especially when they are men you have tested your own wrestling against and can get a rough gauge for your position in the crowd. That had been happening for me all week.

Chris Taylor lost one more close match and had to settle for bronze.

Two Brothers Seek Olympic Medals Together

Things were clear-cut for John. Tediashvili would defeat and eliminate the Romanian John had defeated the night before, and John needed to beat Horst Stottmeister of East Germany. The problem was John had been pinned by Stottmeister in the second period at the World Championships the previous year.

However, John was now a different wrestler with a whole new mindset and was still riding the crest of an incredible learning curve. His confidence, his condition, and his techniques were miles better. He spoke confidently as he prepared for his match. He assured me he could win and get the silver and that I could pin and get the gold. I remember his confidence being contagious. He had turned other results around and he knew he could do it again.

As was often the case, our matches would take place at roughly the same time. John's match started first. Taking control of the tie-ups, he began shooting explosive doubles. He had scored more than once before I even put a foot on my mat. But at that point it was like John and I stepped into separate capsules going to separate planets. He had his job to do and I had mine. I would watch him until it was my time to compete. He would stay totally focused on his match until it was done. Then he would be beside my mat. There was no one we wanted to see win more than each other. Our brotherly rivalry had pushed each of us in practice day after day, but now we were totally supportive of each other.

John continued his relentless tie-up control and double leg barrage while I began my match with Rusi Petrov of Bulgaria. This was the medal round and we were both intense. Each of us knew what was at stake. Tie-ups and takedowns were attempted and hard counters were used by both of us.

Using my left arm I got an underhook on Petrov's right side. After a bit, I tried a bear hug, relying on all the methods my college teammates had hammered me with. I pressed for a fast pace, faster than he wanted. I got the takedown and then had him on his back.

John secured a solid win against Stottmeister and along with it the silver medal! While the referee was raising his hand, John thought of me and turned to my mat to see what was happening. There I was, chest-to-chest, squeezing the Bulgarian to the mat!

John watched my referee's hand go up, signaling the fall. One of the other two officials must agree and they did. I had won! And won by the pin our coaches assured me I could get.

Standing to shake hands with my opponent and then the official, I waited for him to raise my hand. Afterwards, as I began to walk toward the edge of the mat, I was attacked from the side by John. He was so excited! He bear hugged me as we walked over to our coaches waiting for us in the mat corner.

A picture of that embrace was sent all over America. One big-city newspaper after another used that picture. And people from all walks of life and all corners of the nation sent our parents and us complimentary notes along with the picture and the adjoining news article. They expressed pride and appreciation for our victories and many also for our stated faith in Christ.

There were a few short moments of elation for us and then the reality of the setting came to play. John was approached for a random drug test, and he and a coach were taken to the testing site. No delays, no time to celebrate, he was ushered out immediately.

Bill Weick's "ifs" came to mind. I had now forced Gennadi Strakhov, the Soviet, to win by ten or more points to beat me. He was wrestling Karoly Bojko of Hungary. Sitting on the stairway just back from the raised mat platform I began to watch the match all by myself. I was wishing John was there. Where were all the coaches? Why was everyone gone? Then it hit me. Coach Weick had said they would have every U.S. coach reminding the officials to watch the Soviet's match. They believed he would try to pay the Hungarian not to win, but rather let Strakhov win, and win big. However, our coaches believed Strakhov *would* win, but that it would be a good match unless the Hungarian got paid off.

I watched Strakhov talk to his opponent a handful of times during the match. The officials noticed and warned him not to do so. If Bojko and Strakhov obviously threw a match, neither wrestler would get a medal. The Hungarian kept working but the score kept growing. And then time was up. Final score Soviet 9, Hungarian 1!

Apparently, I had now won the gold medal. However, I was still moderately numb by the events of the morning, plus everyone else was still busy with their activities and matches. John wasn't there for almost an hour, the coaches were off with other wrestlers, and I was left somewhat by myself after the Soviet/Hungarian match. Ever since, whenever I have seen Coach Farrell, he has always rehearsed how all his coaches were going around telling the 40+ officials to keep an eye on the Soviet/Hungarian match. Many ignored it and went back to reading their morning newspapers. That made Coach Farrell really mad.

People began to congratulate me throughout the day but it hadn't fully sunk in yet that the gold medal was truly mine. It was early afternoon and the medal ceremony would not take place until early evening. Meanwhile, John was trying to give a urine sample for the drug test. He was so excited and nervous that it took a very long time for him to come up with a sample. After drinking water, Coke, and juice he was finally able to give them what they needed and was told he was okay.

Bad Marks

The "Bad Mark" system is no longer used in wrestling, so let me explain it briefly. Many of you are likely wondering how John won his last match but earned silver, and why I had to pin my final opponent and wait for the results of the Soviet/Hungarian match to win the gold.

We wrestled the other competitors over the course of several days, and at the end of each match a total of four bad marks were handed out. If you got a pin, you got none and your opponent got all four. So, I could win a match decisively and still get a bad mark if I did not win by pin. Tying an opponent resulted in two bad marks for each wrestler, and losing resulted in three for the loser and one for the winner. A ten-point win gave you half a mark and the loser got three and a half marks. Once you accumulated six bad marks you were eliminated.

To make a long story short, I had tied Strakhov of the Soviet Union in an earlier match. Since neither of us had lost a match, it became a race to see who would earn the least marks. I went into that last match with the same number of pins as Strakhov, and that is why I had to pin my last opponent from Bulgaria. Strakhov and I each ended with four marks, and pins would break the tie.

John could only win the silver in his final match because he had already lost to Tediashvili, but could secure the second lowest number of bad marks if he won his final match. Confused? Needless to say, the current system appears simpler.

Two Champions Finish in Style

The rest of the day was intense. There were a lot of smiles and laughter, and we were congratulated by our parents and Phil and everyone else. After lunch, John and I returned for the final evening session. Our weights were done, but Wayne Wells and Dan Gable still needed to wrestle.

Wayne wrestled the first of his two matches that evening and won by fall. Then it was Gable's turn. There were no technical falls back then, and Dan had been scoring over twenty points or winning by pin in every match. Dan started strong, pushing to score and tire the Soviet. Dan scored three takedowns for one point each and took a 3-0 lead.

John and I expected him to keep scoring and rolling past his opponent. Dan never stalled or backed up, but he became more cautious than we had ever seen him wrestle. I think he kept waiting for some special trick from the Soviet. A Soviet wrestling dignitary had vowed they would search the entire Soviet nation to find someone to beat Gable. We, and Dan, were surprised at whom they chose. There was nothing new or special about him. In the end I think they only found someone to look respectable and not quit.

The match ended 3-0. John and I, plus a few others, were nearby watching the match. Gable was completing a seven match shutout against the world's Olympic best. I think it was John who said, "Hey, let's carry Dan off the mat." So we jumped up and ran on the mat to carry him down.

I think we embarrassed Dan. He kept telling us to put him down. Then he said something like, "I came here to win the Olympics. And I did. So put me down." He was so matter-of-fact about it. He had reached his goal and that was his reward. He and his parents could relax now and enjoy it. At that point there was little emotion in Dan's voice.

Later, Dan would get a little choked up when he reflected on how others like John and I also won medals. He took obvious pride and joy in our success and so did his parents. Two months later I stopped by their house in Waterloo when Kate Gable was home. We talked about Munich and laughed and smiled a lot. Then she said to me, "Ben, I'll bet you haven't stopped smiling since you won that gold medal." And I don't think she had stopped smiling either!

Wayne Wells still needed to wrestle one more match, his third of the day. Wayne's sore ribs and his deep resolve would be stretched one more time. He could lose the match, yet still win gold because of his previous wins and pins. The arena was full of people and full of energy since Wayne was wrestling the West German, Adolf Seger. Seger had lost one match already so he would have to pin Wayne to get the gold. Many German athletes from other sports were in attendance and cheering for Adolf.

Wayne clearly was the best on his feet, getting early takedowns. But more than once Adolf reversed Wayne to take away the point and the momentum. It would have been easy for Wayne to be content to let his determined opponent win. The crowd kept giving Seger energy, creating an emotional charge around the match. But Wayne, the determined young man with American pride, could not go out losing. Wayne's exhaustion was clearly evident, yet he repeatedly fought back to another takedown. Finally, he secured the victory and the gold medal with just seconds left. To me, Wayne has symbolized a determined willingness to represent the USA with guts and class.

The Emotional Roller Coaster Continues

Finally it was time to receive our medals. John got his medal first. What a sight it was to see him standing there receiving his Olympic silver medal! What an improvement he had made in such a short time. And what an encouragement he is to all young wrestlers who have not yet reached their potential. His determination sitting on a Comstock tractor had not lagged more than a few days for thirteen and a half months. I felt extremely proud of him and so did all the rest of America.

Then it was my turn. Getting on the medal stand first before the other place winners and receiving the gold was a surprise. In America, we always start at the lesser award and then go up to first place. I nervously greeted Strakhov and then Bojko, shaking hands and nodding with a smile. They gave little positive reaction in response.

Suddenly, as the flags began to be raised, the first bars of The Star Spangled Banner filled the arena. Listening to the other country's anthems had been depressing, but it had not occurred to me they would play the U.S. national anthem, and a surreal question came to mind: "Why are they playing our beautiful national anthem?" With a smile I thought, "Thank you, God. You let me win a few silly wrestling matches and my whole nation is being honored."

Then my thoughts went to the significance of this night and that my life would have many changes. I knew life would never be the same and that others would look at me differently.

My frustrating time after winning the NCAA Championships came to mind. I had asked that wrestling victory to solve all my problems and change me as a person. I now lowered my head briefly, looked at the gold medal and said to God, "You can have this medal. It is yours. I don't want to hoard the attention for myself." Then I looked back up at the flag and enjoyed the rest of The Star Spangled Banner.

Coming off the podium, I was informed there was a box for the medal waiting for me. While I was heading to get the box, Coach Peckham joined me with a big smile and put his arm around my shoulders. He looked at the medal and said, **"It is all yours now. They can never take it away from you!"**

I thought of the events of that day. I thought of needing to get a pin against the Bulgarian and then watching the Soviet talk to the Hungarian. I remembered how our coaches were working to keep the officials watching the match. People had congratulated me all day, but I had not yet received the medal.

Now I had the medal! Coach Peckham's statement and my thoughts were too much; I broke down and cried like a baby. I remember the tears being so intense I could not see where we were going and had to stop and wipe them away.

Those were tears of joy without a doubt, but also of relief. All the dreaming and all the pressure we had put on ourselves was now relieved. I think it all hit me at that moment. Coach's confirmation also caused incredible thankfulness to well up inside. I wanted to thank everyone: my teammates, our coaches, the Gables, my family, and many more right then and there. And then I wanted to thank God. It seemed so spectacular that John and I could actually win a gold and a silver medal in Munich, Germany, in 1972.

John and I have been thanking God and all those who helped us ever since. We also enjoy thanking Americans we do not even know, including you. A country is made up of its people, and we received so much support from people we had never met. In turn, John and I experienced the incredible motivation of taking on the responsibility and opportunity of representing the people of America. What a privilege it was to represent the USA in that event!

I recall the team getting together for pictures. There was a lot of smiling with our three gold medals, two silvers, and a bronze: that was more medals than any U.S. Olympic wrestling team had ever earned. Yet there was disappointment for the four without medals. And we also knew the Soviet team was well ahead of us with five golds.

See Appendix C - The Big Stage Does Not Always Equal Vivid Memories

—38—

EXTREME MUNICH MEMORIES AND THE ADVENT OF MODERN TERRORISM

Standing on the victory stand in Munich, Germany, the thought hit me that a major change would be happening in my life. Some great memories would always go with me.

After coming down from the medal ceremony, Coach Peckham's statement, "They can never take it away from you now," reinforced the fact that things would change. I did not really comprehend what all the changes would be, but at least I knew John and I would no longer be just another pair of wrestlers trying to do their best. We would have our own memories of the competition and preparation, and now many others would also have vivid memories of our accomplishments.

Memories of the Bavarian mountains and quaint villages would be etched in our minds as well. John and I spent three days south of Munich in the town of Oberammergau where most of the American wrestler's parents were housed. They had bed and breakfast arrangements in several private homes.

Being a tourist in a foreign land gave us a glimpse of where many American immigrants had come from. A visit to a castle and the mountain home of Ludwig, Mad King of Bavaria, showed wealth, kingship, and power over others like America never experienced. Those three days were also a relaxing time where the reality of our Olympic medals began to sink in.

Chris Taylor and his family joined us for one day of touring. That day confirmed why Chris was so much fun. His parents and sisters all added to the joking and entertainment. His dad was the best at it. We laughed continually even while climbing mountains to visit the sites. Afterwards, I regret that Chris walked so much with us in those mountains. Carrying his 425 pounds was a tiring task for him.

But he did not want to be left behind and miss his dad's jokes, and he did not want to lose the chance to tell his own stories. Father and son created memories our parents commented about for twenty years.

Then it was back to Munich. We scheduled a museum tour of the city for the next day with our parents and Phil and Rita. Our meeting time was under the Glockenspiel (animated clock) at 9:00 a.m. to watch the famous clock perform on the hour.

As we woke up that morning there were rumors about some trouble in the Olympic Village. When Dan Gable came back from his morning run, he talked about the tight security at the gate. John and I hurried on our way to get breakfast in the Village cafeteria before touring. We took a shortcut through the garage area. John saw an armored vehicle and commented, "What is that doing in the Olympic Village?!" While eating breakfast, someone pointed down a certain walkway to various apartments and said, "Don't go that way, it's blocked off." We had no need to go in that part of the Village since we were going out the main gate in the opposite direction. After finishing breakfast we headed to the gate and train stop to get a ride downtown. I do not recall hearing anything more about problems in the Village. We were set on seeing the history and grandeur of Munich.

After meeting our parents at "the clock" we headed off to a museum. Phil had staked out the key museums and planned a timeline to view each one. We saw the glory of past kings and we saw the history of Germany. And then we saw the horror of World War II. The strongest memory of the city was seeing whole city blocks still in ruins from the war. We voiced our surprise at seeing so much untouched while everything else in the city was built and decorated so nicely with the Olympic theme.

Phil recalled Germany's decision to leave whole blocks untouched to remind the next generation of the horror of the war. The impression and emotions from suddenly passing those decimated city blocks immediately after walking through a modern well-built city has been strong in my mind ever since.

At the Engineering Museum, John heard about Olympic events being postponed. We brushed it off as "nothing stops the Olympics" and continued our sightseeing.

After concluding our touring, John and I headed to the

wrestling site to watch the Greco-Roman team compete. To our amazement we found the doors locked and a sign on the door in multiple languages saying the competition was postponed. We exclaimed, "What?! The Olympics are postponed? Nothing can stop the Olympics!"

Turning away in our wonderment we saw my college coach, Harold Nichols and his wife, Ruth, step out of a taxi. We told Coach about the sign. He had been touring during the day also, but he had heard about Olympic Village troubles that included a break-in.

After talking a bit with Coach Nichols, John and I headed to the subway to ride back to the Village for the night. Working our way toward an escalator, a paperboy called out in German the news of the day. He could see I was an American, and as I walked by, he pushed the paper in front of me and insisted something I could not understand.

I was hurrying to keep up with John and the other Americans and I thought, "It's a German paper and I can't read it. No need to stop." Looking back, I think the boy had a paper in English and knew I would be able to read the "big news" of the day.

When we arrived at the Village, the courtyard outside the main gate was filled with people talking very intently in small groups. Grasping bits of news from other English-speaking athletes and coaches, we began to piece together the story of terrorists breaking into the Village and capturing eleven members of the Israeli contingent. Some of these were wrestlers, weightlifters, and coaches.

Joining with a couple other wrestlers, we decided to go to another gate around the back of the Village. John recalls walking on the sidewalk several yards from the Village fence with the German National Guard standing side by side all along the fence. That really sobered him. He realized at that point that something very serious had happened. The friendly Olympic Village was now an armored camp.

As we worked our way through a service entry we found ourselves walking through the underground driveways and parking lots. There were no streets or vehicles above ground in the Village, only walkways.

Arriving upstairs in our apartment we learned relatively new words like "Palestinian" and "terrorists." The Israelis had been captured and taken to the airport by the terrorists. We gathered what we could from the coverage that was in English, and were told the terrorists and Israelis were killed at the airport. It would be a while before more details were available and more of the story was told of how the terrorists had demanded helicopters in order to take the Israelis away. While at the airport, the terrorists thwarted the German ambush attempt by using grenades on the Israelis before being killed themselves. Of the massacre, only two terrorists survived.

Phil and Rita traveled to Vienna that night and flew back home, gathering information as they went. Phil concluded, **"This is a horrible thing. It will change the Olympics and the world forever."** And he was right. Piecing together all the smaller and bigger events of the day would take weeks.

Soon after, I was on a plane heading back to the U.S. The fall semester at Iowa State had started and I was missing critical class time of my final quarter before graduation. John would come later. It was the first time all summer we had been apart. The Games were over and it was time to get back to responsibilities.

But some things had changed. Congratulations repeatedly came for winning the Olympic medals. It seemed every American was proud of our successes. It was very rewarding to see how happy people were for us. John and I seemed to have put a big smile in the hearts of a lot of people and that thought was rewarding from the start.

Mark Spitz had won seven gold medals in swimming, and every American was also rejoicing with him. We were frequently asked if we saw him. John remembers seeing him on the plane from Washington D.C. to Munich. Spitz sat a few rows ahead of him and impressed John with his good-natured laugh and kidding around. He knew how to relax before the battle; a very important ability for athletes at that level of competition. Mark Spitz was the Michael Phelps of the Munich Olympics, and until Phelps accomplished what he has, every noteworthy swimming victory was compared to Spitz.

Another question kept coming to us and still does. "Were you close to the terrorists? What about the Israelis?" Our answer is we did not know as much as the average American did watching their TV until it was all over and we were able to get hold of English news. Our Olympic apartment was a couple hundred yards away and there was a ten-story building between us. We never felt unsafe, but we also did not know the significance until it was over.

That event began the "terrorist age," where a few could get the attention of the whole world just by threatening the right people. In today's media, and especially after 9-11, most Americans are aware of terrorism. We know what it is, the people who protect us study how to watch for it, and in most cases prevent it without us even knowing it. As a nation, we have experienced getting back to work and play while we trust the men and women of the law enforcement and military systems to keep us safe.

But back then, while wars and fighting between people groups was very much a reality, nobody had really used such a public stage to make their point. They handled their quarrels "on the ground," away from the rest of the world. Because of this, even a nation as strong and as well-trained militarily as Germany was not fully prepared for what hit them. And the world was not well prepared for the psychological effect of the news either.

In 1982, John attended an Olympic conference in Boden Boden, Germany. The theme was "Peace Through and By Sport." John left thinking that sports cannot bring lasting world peace. Maybe it can help for a brief period as athletes like us cross social and political lines, but he knew that only Jesus Christ brings true lasting peace. And true peace is in the hearts of individuals until Christ comes again to bring lasting peace.

Another event of those Olympics was the U.S. basketball team's loss to the Soviets. On the night flight back to America, I heard people talking about the loss where the last few seconds were played multiple times until the Soviets scored. What a negative, puzzling event that was!

While John and I returned excited and pleased with our medals and the wrestling team's improved performance, we lived with a severe mixture of negatives and positives. We soon learned that the mention of Munich could bring all Americans to talk of American medals, but it would also lead to thoughts of the massacre and the first ever U.S. basketball loss. Back and forth these memories would be sifted through our minds and all who spoke to us. We became a point of memory for others for extreme highs and lows, which is like most of life. **Every period of human history has its positive and negative aspects. We learned to live with both of them.**

—39—
WELCOME HOME!

When we arrived home in early September, our small hometown of Comstock greeted us in grand fashion. Our welcome could not have been any better. It made both of us proud to call Comstock our home.

A couple days into my studies at ISU I received a call: Comstock wants me to come home for a welcome back celebration. John had been back for a day, and we met with others to form a motorcade at a city park in Clear Lake, about twenty miles southwest of Comstock. Nearly forty vehicles made up the motorcade that night. Mom, Dad, John, and I all rode in the motorcade, and Wisconsin Governor Patrick Lucey was there, too.

The motorcade left Clear Lake and traveled north on U.S. Highway 63 toward Comstock. We passed through the small communities of Richardson, Clayton, and Turtle Lake. Then we drove right on through Comstock without stopping, past the feed mill where Dad worked and the tractors John and I had sat on for pivotal conversations, travelling to Cumberland, where we had gone to high school and had gotten our start in wrestling. The motorcade made a loop around Cumberland and then returned to Comstock.

For miles along the route from Clear Lake to Cumberland to Comstock, people were everywhere cheering for us, waving to us, and welcoming us home. We heard sirens and fireworks along the way.

When the motorcade ride ended, we were right in the middle of a hayfield on the edge of Comstock near the town hall. It was one of Stanley and Lilly Jergenson's hayfields, newly mowed just in time for our welcome home. Stanley and Lilly and their family were longtime friends of ours and it felt good to go from the Olympic medal stand to the hayfield of good down-home friends.

Comstock Says Welcome Home

Many from Comstock and the surrounding communities came out for the occasion in Jergenson's hayfield. It was 8:00 or 8:30 p.m. when we arrived and the power company had put up a number of lighted poles throughout the hayfield. The gas company had placed a burner nearby to simulate the Olympic flame, and a big tent was pitched for use if it rained.

With the help of others in the community, Stanley had built a platform as a podium especially for the evening. John and I, Mom and Dad, Governor Lucey, Coach Walsh, Stanley, and others were seated on the platform. John and I wore our official white Olympic blazers, red slacks, and red, white, and blue ties. And I suppose we wore our Olympic medals too!

The crowd that gathered was reported by the *Milwaukee Journal* to be somewhere between 1,000 and 1,500 people. The Associated Press ("AP") reported that local law enforcement (Barron County Sheriff Wally Larson) estimated the crowds including the motorcade route to be 4,000 or maybe even 5,000 people. As we all walked up together and sat down on the platform, the sound that we heard all around us was deafening. We heard cheering and shouting, and everywhere we looked we saw big smiles.

Then the program began. First, the Cumberland High School band played several patriotic selections and The Star Spangled Banner was sung. Stanley introduced Governor Lucey who said the "entire nation can be proud of these gentle, strong men" from Comstock. Then he officially declared September 13, 1972, as "John and Ben Peterson Day in all of Wisconsin."

Our wrestling coach, Jack Walsh, spoke next. He said some really nice things about us for which we were both grateful. After Coach Walsh spoke, the Gamble Folk Singers from Minneapolis sang several gospel and folk songs.

Next was Comstock's oldest citizen, Martin Tyvoll, who was 83. Martin had owned and operated the General Store in Comstock for decades. He presented John and me with large gold "Keys to Comstock." No one had ever received a key to Comstock before, and we were thrilled to be the first.

Then it was our turn to speak to the crowd. But words were not nearly enough to describe just how John and I really felt about all that had happened to us. We both said thank you; thank you to Comstock for this fantastic welcome home, which really surprised us; and thank you to everyone there that night for all that Comstock, our home, had meant to us over the years. We were both honored to represent the United States of America and honored to represent Comstock in the 1972 Munich Olympics.

We thanked Mom and Dad and the rest of our family. We also thanked Coach Walsh for the good start he had given us in wrestling. Finally, we emphasized just how important our faith in Jesus Christ was to us. We simply thanked God for the stability and value of His Word and for blessing our efforts.

Last on the program was the pastor of our home church, Reverend Donald Toney, who gave the benediction.

After the program concluded, we talked and talked to many people who were there to greet us. First we talked to the press, and then we talked late into the night to anyone else who wanted to. We talked to friends and neighbors among whom we had lived for all those years growing up. And we talked to many strangers whom we met for the first time. It was a wonderful evening, and one we will never forget!

A newspaper reporter showed John the picture of us hugging when our Olympic competition was over and we had won our medals. The reporter asked, "John, is that the greatest thing that's ever happened to you?"

Before answering the question, John thought for a moment. Then he replied, "Well, for sure, it was a great thing. But it wasn't the 'greatest thing that ever happened to me.' The 'greatest thing' happened when I was just twelve years old, and I gave my life to Jesus Christ." John is thankful God gave him the courage to declare that night that God is more important in his life than Olympic medals. Since then, it has been reassuring to know that his relationship with Christ doesn't depend on what he has done. Rather, his relationship with God is made secure because of what Jesus did when He died on the cross in our place. He has learned how important it is to be trusting daily in Christ as personal Lord and Savior.

What a Terrific Welcome Home

The *Milwaukee Journal,* the largest circulating newspaper in

Wisconsin, sent a news reporter all the way to Comstock, 315 miles northwest of Milwaukee, to cover the event. The front page story the next day was datelined "Comstock," and it began as follows:

> "They *wrote the book* here Wednesday night on how to welcome home Olympic heroes.
>
> In this little unincorporated Barron County community of about 75 people, they put it all together and welcomed home the Peterson brothers with *warmth and style.*
>
> It was a *classy celebration* from the time Comstock citizens got the word from Munich and began preparations."

John and I agree entirely! Indeed, Comstock "wrote the book" that night on how to carry out a classy celebration. What a tremendous welcome home it was for both of us, planned and carried out to perfection by those who have known us the longest and the best.

What makes this more interesting is the fact the entire event was planned and carried out by three unlikely men: a forty-cow dairy farmer, a small implement/auto dealer, and a cheese factory owner. They were the leaders of that unincorporated village and were friends of our parents. These were not the people you would think would create such an event. But they sure knew what they were doing. And the timing and everyone's excitement made it a very special and unique homecoming.

FINAL NOTE

My hope is that this book encourages you in your own life. If, as you read, you can learn from our ups and downs, my purpose will be met. It is an honor to help others.

With God's help and the encouragement of others, I hope to tell more of our story. I would like to write about what life has been like for John and me since 1972 when we won our medals in the Munich Olympics. And I would like to write about us winning a second gold and a second silver medal in the 1976 Olympics in Montreal.

I would like to tell our readers how winning Olympic medals affected our lives and how we stayed motivated to continue wrestling for the United States for eight more years after the Munich Olympics. And I would like to describe how, for over forty years since then, John and I have remained strong in our Christian faith and enthusiastic advocates for wrestling.

I look forward to your reaction to this first book, and am most pleased to have it available to many interested readers.

If you have questions or areas that you hope to see written about in the future, please email me at ben@campofchamps.org. I hope to encourage you and others with additional stories. But those must wait for another day.

May God bless you in your efforts to develop your talents and make your own road to gold.

Ben Peterson

Munich Village 1972.

Opening ceremonies with Gene Davis and John.

Me, Mack, Katie Gable, and John at the Olympic Village.

Mom, Dad, and Phil with John and me.

Ruth and Coach Harold Nichols with us in Munich.

John, Mom, Dad and me between sessions.

John, Chris, and me visiting a Bavarian village.

Holding John down for lifting at the Olympic Village.

Coach Jack Walsh takes a picture of me, Dan and John at the Olympic training camp at the University of Minnesota.

Countering a leg attack from my favorite freestyle position.

Doing a power double in Munich - *photo taken by J Robinson.*

John working a double against Peter Neumair of West Germany in his second match.

Working for an opening.

Walking off the mat with John after our simultaneous wins.

Tediashvili leading a friendly gesture.

Receiving the gold medal.

Tent, platform and flags in Stanley Jergenson's hayfield.

Strakhov from USSR, me, and Bajko from Hungary.

John, Tediashvili (USSR), and Iorga (Romania) on the medal stand.

The 6 freestyle medalists. I was comfortable in a foreign country with these men.

Above: Listening to our National Anthem. Right: John (left) offers his congratulations after our final victories.

'Gentle strongmen,' wide as woodsheds

Members of the1972 US Olympic Freestyle Wrestling Team (front row, from left) Don Behm alternate at 125.5: Sergio Gonzales 105.5, Jimmy Carr 114.5, Rick Sanders 125, Gene Davis 136.5, Dan Gable 149.5, Wayne Wells 163, Team Manager Russ Houck. (back row, from left) Head Coach Bill Farrell, our assigned medical person, John 180.5, Ben 198, Henk Schenk 220, Chris Taylor heavyweight, Assistant Coach Jim Peckham, Assistant Coach Bill Weick.

Above: Munich Olympic medalists - John 180.5 silver, Wayne Wells 163 gold, Ben 198 gold, Chris Taylor heavyweight bronze, Dan Gable 149.5 gold, and Rick Sanders 125 silver.

Above: All smiles with 1972 gold medal.

Right: 1972 Olympic Gold Medal.

Welcome home with Governor Patrick Lucey, Mom, and Dad.

Mom and Dad proudly displaying our keys to Comstock.

APPENDIX A

Set Up the Lines of Defense

There are five lines of defense that God gave John and me in dealing with any distraction or temptation:

1. **Our conscience:** As I would think about things, my conscience would often inform me of right and wrong. A conscience needs instruction, reminders, and support, making the following vital.

2. **Family:** In our case, our family was a big factor. We had worked diligently together on our farm. We played intently and knew and cared deeply for each other. I still have an eight-inch stack of letters my family sent to me while I was at Iowa State. How could I do things I knew they were saying no to? And how could I face Mom and Becky knowing I had acted selfishly in a relationship with a young woman?

3. **The Scriptures:** I had been taught the truth. I knew what was right and wrong. A standard older, much wiser than I, and as respected as the Bible is worth listening to.

4. **The Holy Spirit:** *"Do you not know that you are the temple of God, and that the Spirit of God dwells in you?" I Corinthians 3:16* This verse is an encouragement for those who trust Jesus Christ as their Savior from sin. The Holy Spirit indwells us. We need to learn to listen and be led by God through His Spirit.

5. **Local church:** A group of believers in Christ can be an encouragement to avoid sin. When you study and discuss God's truths and promises with other Christians, it will give backbone to your knowledge and confidence in your convictions. Wherever John and I have travelled we have looked for a group of believers that gathers to worship the Lord, learn about Him, and tell others of God's incredible mercy.

With these five lines of defense, John and I have avoided dangers in many areas. And when we made mistakes, we knew where to go for forgiveness and to strengthen the defense for the next temptations.

APPENDIX B

Choosing a Greater Good *by: Andy Peterson*

This part of the story does not really revolve around magazines, movies or the internet, even though thoughts naturally determine attitudes and actions. Just as with the chapter on alcohol and other substances, the real issues revolve around how we choose to satisfy different urges within us.

We do not question discomforts during wrestling training once we envision ourselves experiencing hard-earned wrestling success. This is because we can feel the positive end emotions ahead of time. Yet it is fairly natural for us as humans to question limitations of any kind when we cannot anticipate the positive emotions that await those who are willing to follow God's designed pattern for enjoyment.

I believe God gave us His Word, not only to draw us into a relationship with Him, but to give us the "cheat sheet" for the most enjoyable life possible. After all, He designed pleasure in all areas of life. But don't just take my word, or anyone else's word. Read it for yourself. In Proverbs and Song of Solomon you will find more than enough evidence that God smiles on those who enjoy His gifts in a self-sacrificing, loving, trust-filled relationship as opposed to a self-indulgent, impatient, single-focused one.

Various forms of media and segments of society have relegated a man's potentially vast and unfathomable experience of a woman to ink on a page or streaming digital bytes that are cheap and easy. Nothing about this shallow transaction of attaining sexual satisfaction fits with the model God intended, where deep love and commitment is invested long before the physical unity of marriage and sex.

It only makes sense many young people mention fear of getting bored with a single marriage relationship when everything they know about sensuality is shallow and commitment-free rather than the single, always discovering and deepening kind of relationship God designed for a man and a woman.

Now that I am married to a similarly committed woman, I have found the old cliché to be true: marriage only gets better with time.

APPENDIX C

The Big Stage Does Not Always Equal Vivid Memories

Oddly enough, the original writing about the Olympic matches was significantly shorter than it is now. It was short in the beginning because there are several matches I have little memory of. Many of my memories from childhood, high school, and college are more vivid than my Olympic memories. My family and friends thought I should add to this chapter. I had to use partial videos and the historical records of my match scores to help me with more details of several matches.

Andy and I talked about why that might be. In the end, he came up with the following explanations, and you might find them helpful as you chase your own expectations in life, especially athletics. Others who have been blessed with similar high points seem to share the realization that what others see as superlative events do not always provide the same vivid memories for themselves. My match with the Iranian is a prime example. For years, I have had no memory of it.

The following are in no particular order since every person's reasons are likely to be different.

• **Rationing adrenaline.** Many long-term athletes have learned to control their emotions. In addition to purposely controlling emotional responses, experienced athletes also understand how to ration their adrenaline and energy levels. There is nothing more memory-enhancing than a big shot of adrenaline and experienced athletes have learned how to keep their adrenaline levels stable. They have learned to allow short bursts of adrenaline that get the immediate job done while not allowing so much that the adrenaline gets them out of control or overly fatigued. There are exceptions of course. For instance, I vividly remember the scramble with Russ Hellickson when I finally defeated him with a pin. But, it was not memorable because I pinned him: it was the huge shot of adrenaline released when I realized how out of position I was! The "fight or flight" response really kicked in and I just happened to be able to recover faster than Russ did.

• **The thrill of the new** is also a big contributor to vivid memories. Scientists are beginning to prove that there are few, if any, experiences in life more memorable and even pleasurable, than the moment of learning something new. It does not matter if it is in the classroom, in the practice room, or with someone you are learning more about. When you say "aha, that makes sense," or "wow, I never knew that before," your brain files away not just the "aha" lesson, but also a lot of the details of your surroundings and the situation. It's like a dog getting a treat. It wants to recreate the situation because it assumes the treat will come again. But when it does, it is not as memorable because the dog did not experience anything new. By the time a wrestler gets to the Olympics, there are not a lot of new experiences, even on the mat.

Seldom do you see Olympians doing anything overly complicated. They are doing the same move the same way they have done it thousands of times. If they remember anything about a particular takedown, it is more likely to be a setup they had to improvise against that particular competitor rather than the actual takedown.

Many coaches make sure their wrestlers have a chance to roll around on the mats right after they get to a new gym rather than waiting until right before the official starting time. This gives the brain a chance to process the surroundings, including the mat surface, placement of clocks, and anything else that might be a new experience and distracting during the match. If given enough time to adjust, the mind should find everything about the surroundings completely boring by match time, leaving it to focus solely on the puzzle presented by the opponent.

- **Picturing success** is a two-edged sword. There is a significant rise in books and coaches that suggest taking time to visualize what success will feel like, what it will look like, and what it will take to get there. While this has been proven through much research to significantly increase the odds of accomplishing what you imagine, it also takes away some of the "thrill of the new." It can also cause disappointment if the accomplishment does not live up to your expectations. Many champions report feeling less emotion immediately after their actual success because they had imagined it so vividly many times before. And not just the emotions and how it would feel, but how they would do it. How they might set up and finish their best takedown, or how they would control the pace to match their type of conditioning rather than their opponent's.

• **Life moves on -** especially after the Olympics where there was a whirlwind of celebration and then back to normal life. After success in high school, John and I would day-dream about our experiences and even retell them like fishermen do with big fish stories. Everything was so fresh and new and we were still figuring out the sport, so there was much to learn and relearn and talk about. After the Olympics, we had a lot of other thoughts going through our heads, not to mention significantly more responsibilities taking up our time.

We were trained to look forward. When we were younger wrestlers, we simply spent more time thinking about the past. We still did this as older wrestlers, but not in the same way. We would think about a match or a situation long enough to get the lesson, and then move our focus to the next challenge more quickly than when we were younger. This was especially true in the Olympics, where every single competitor in the tournament was a serious challenge and we knew we could not dwell on our past match.

• **Other things in life were just as thrilling and important,** even if in a different way. Wrestling was obviously one of our top priorities, but we had experienced many thrilling moments outside of wrestling as well. When asked by a reporter if the Olympics was the greatest moment in his life, John could honestly answer that trusting Jesus Christ was a bigger moment for him. In addition to high points in our faith, we would both be moving on with coaching and eventually having a family.

• **We did not expect the Olympics to "fix us."** We appreciated the experience for what it was, but not more than we knew it could give. We both knew that being an Olympic medalist would change the trajectory of our lives, but we had developed a better sense of what those changes would not include. I briefly mentioned earlier that the months after my first NCAA championship were some of the most miserable of my life. I had projected all kinds of expectations onto that accomplishment that it could not bring about. Sure, other people would look at me differently, but somewhere in the back of my mind I had allowed myself to wish that winning a championship would fix other things about me. I subconsciously expected it to make me less shy, help me with my studies, and give me more boldness when sharing my faith. In short, I thought an accomplishment in wrestling would fix things about me that I could only fix by changing habits or by the help of God. And frankly, I needed to accept that some things about me needed to be appreciated for what they already were.

As you read this segment, I hope you found more than just musings and ramblings. I hope you also found some ideas that can help you reach your own mountain-top experiences and handle them in stride.

I am thankful that in just the last several years, John was given some new footage of some of our matches. This was very helpful as we clarified and corrected some of our memories.

If anyone has our first round and our final matches in Munich we would love to see them.

My grandson, William, helping proof the book - he approves!